basix

Guitar Method Complete

Ron Manus
Morty Manus

Get Down to BASIX!

BASIX is all you need to take off with your instrument. Alfred has worked hard to help you begin learning today with our easy-to-use, comprehensive series. It won't frustrate you by moving too fast, or let you get bored by moving too slow! You'll notice pics of many great performers; we added those to fire your imagination and help you stay focused on becoming a star yourself! To top it off, you can put what you learn to work when you play along with the companion MP3 CD. Set your sights high by beginning with BASIX... the series that will get you there!

To access the MP3s on the CD, place the CD in your computer's CD-ROM drive. In Windows, double-click on My Computer, then right-click on the CD icon labeled "Basix Guitar Complete" and select Explore to view the files and copy them to your hard drive. For Macs, double-click on the CD icon on your desktop labeled "Basix Guitar Complete" to view the files and copy them to your hard drive.

Alfred Music Publishing Co., Inc.
P.O. Box 10003
Van Nuys, CA 91410-0003
alfred.com

ISBN-10: 0-7390-6245-X (Book & CD)
ISBN-13: 978-0-7390-6245-6 (Book & CD)

Cover photos: Martin Guitar Company (Acoustic) • Fender Musical Instruments, Scottsdale, Arizona (Electric)

Contents: Part 1

Contents: Part 2

Contents: Part 3

Contents: Part 4

The Guitar Parts

The Round Sound Hole or Flat Top Guitar

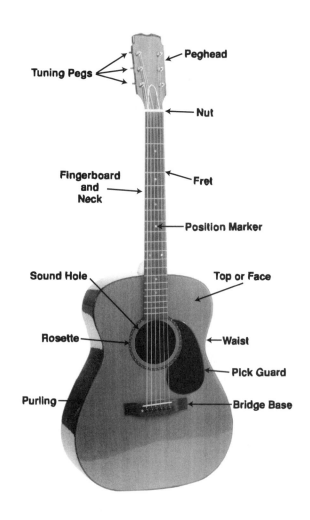

Peghead

Tuning Pegs

Nut

Fret

Fingerboard and Neck

Position Marker

Sound Hole

Top or Face

Rosette

Waist

Pick Guard

Purling

Bridge Base

The Electric Guitar

SEMI-HOLLOW BODY

Tuning Pegs

Position Marker

Cut-away

Upper Bout

Magnetic Pick-ups

F Hole

Toggle Switch

Bridge

Volume Controls

Tone Controls

Arched Top

SOLID BODY

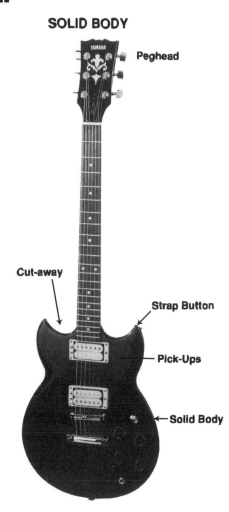

Peghead

Cut-away

Strap Button

Pick-Ups

Solid Body

How to Hold Your Guitar

Hold your guitar in a position which is most comfortable for you.
Some positions are shown below.

When playing, keep your left wrist away from the fingerboard. This will allow your fingers to be in a better position to finger the chords. Press your fingers firmly, but make certain they do not touch the neighboring strings.

The guitar is strummed with the right hand. You may use a guitar pick or your thumb. Strum all chords in a downward motion unless otherwise indicated.

How to Tune Your Guitar

The six strings of your guitar are the same pitch as the
six notes shown on the piano in the following illustration:

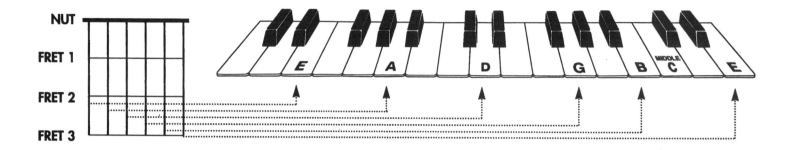

Other Ways of Tuning Your Guitar

Tune the 6th string to E on the piano. If no piano is available,
approximate E as best you can and proceed as follows:

Press 5th fret of 6th string to get pitch of 5th string (A).

Press 5th fret of 5th string to get pitch of 4th string (D).

Press 5th fret of 4th string to get pitch of 3rd string (G).

Press 4th fret of 3rd string to get pitch of 2nd string (B).

Press 5th fret of 2nd string to get pitch of 1st string (E).

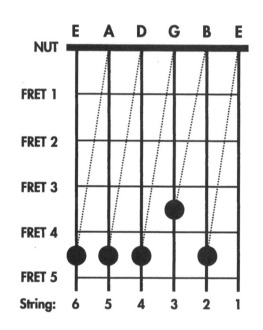

Guitar Diagrams

When introducing the single notes of the guitar, two
diagrams are used. One diagram is used to show the
correct finger position of the note on the guitar fingerboard
along with its musical notation. The other diagram is a
review of all the notes introduced on the page and also the
correct fingering for each note.

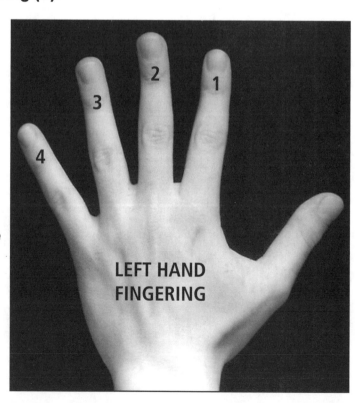

LEFT HAND
FINGERING

Getting Acquainted with Music

Musical sounds are indicated by symbols called NOTES. Their time value is determined by their color (white or black) and by stems and flags attached to the note:

The notes are named after the first seven letters of the alphabet (A-G), endlessly repeated to embrace the entire range of musical sound. The name and pitch of the note is determined by its position on five horizontal lines, and the spaces between, called the...

Staff (Stave)

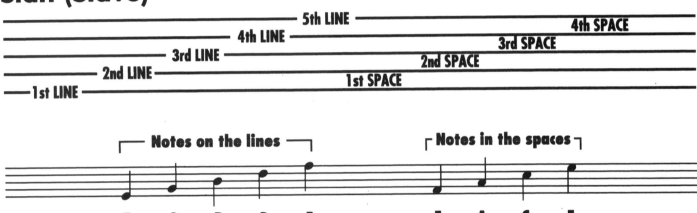

Music is also divided into equal parts, called...

Measures (Bars)

One measure is divided from another by a BAR LINE

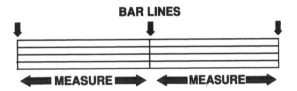

During the evolution of musical notation, the staff had from 2 to 20 lines, and symbols were invented to locate certain lines and the pitch of the note on that line. These symbols were called ...

Clefs

Music for the guitar is written in the G or treble clef. Originally the Gothic letter G was used on a four-line staff to establish the pitch of G:

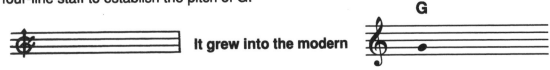

It grew into the modern

Notes on the First String E

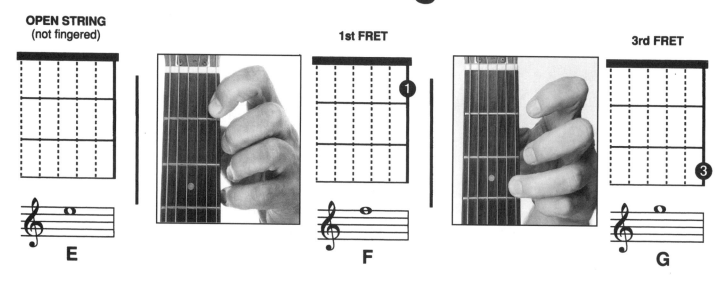

OPEN STRING
(not fingered)

1st FRET

3rd FRET

E   F   G

Dotted line means string is not to be played.

PLAY SLOWLY AND EVENLY—Use only the down-stroke indicated by ⊓.

Go to next line without stopping.

(HOLD)

Playing with E, F, G

DOUBLE BAR LINE

USED AT THE END OF A PIECE

* o means OPEN STRING. Do not finger.

More

Left hand fingers: When playing from the 1st to the 3rd fret, keep the 1st finger down. Only the G will sound, but when you go back to F, your playing will sound smoother.

Still More

Left hand fingers: Place as close to the fret wires as possible without actually touching them.

No More

Left hand fingers: Use only the tips—keep them curved. Left hand thumb: Place on the back of the neck opposite the 1st and 2nd fingers.

Dave Pirner of Soul Asylum has developed a large following of alternative rock fans who respond to his emotional approach to songwriting and guitar playing.

Photo: Amy Lehman © 1995

Dave Pirner *(Soul Asylum)*

Sound-Off: How to Count Time

4 Kinds of Notes

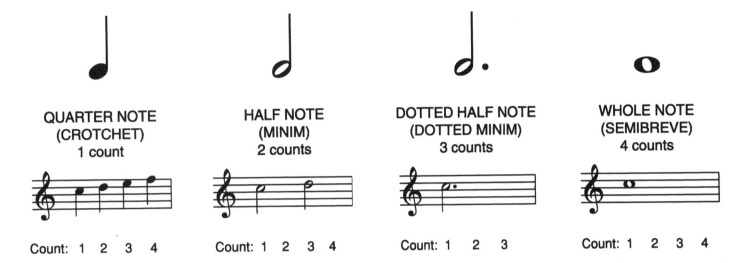

Time Signatures

Each piece of music has numbers at the beginning called a time signature. These numbers tell us how to count time.

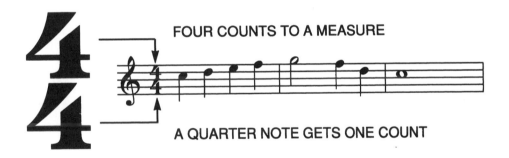

FOUR COUNTS TO A MEASURE

A QUARTER NOTE GETS ONE COUNT

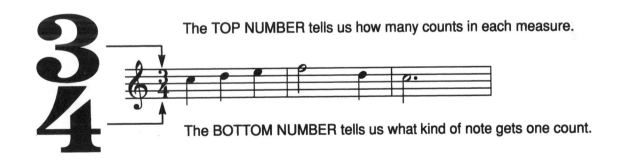

The TOP NUMBER tells us how many counts in each measure.

The BOTTOM NUMBER tells us what kind of note gets one count.

IMPORTANT: Fill in the missing time signatures of the songs already learned.

14

Notes on the Second String B

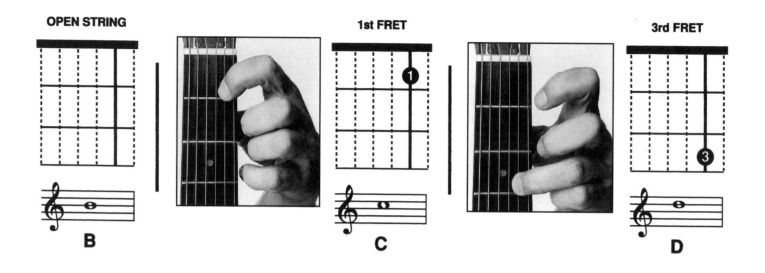

(HOLD 1 DOWN)

Two-String Rock

Merry-Go-Round

Use down-strokes only until further notice.

Beautiful Brown Eyes

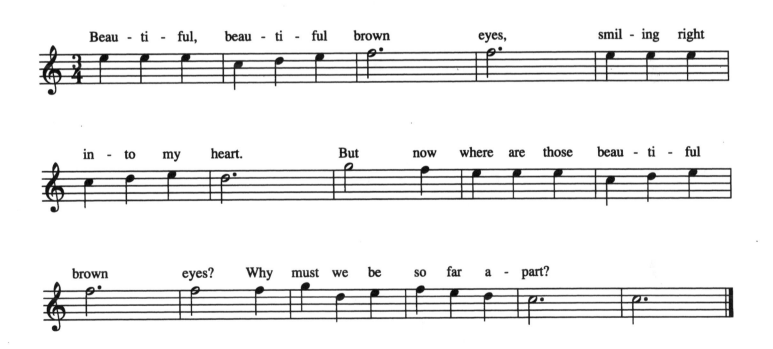

Guitar Rock

If the teacher wishes to play along with the student, the chord symbols above each staff may be used for a teacher-student duet. These chords are not to be played by the student.

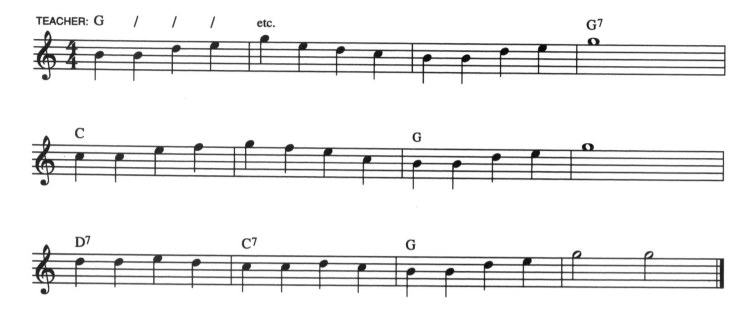

The Ramones were one of the true founders of punk rock, and Johnny Ramone's relentless, straight-ahead style of guitar playing helped shape this sound.

Johnny Ramone

Jingle Bells

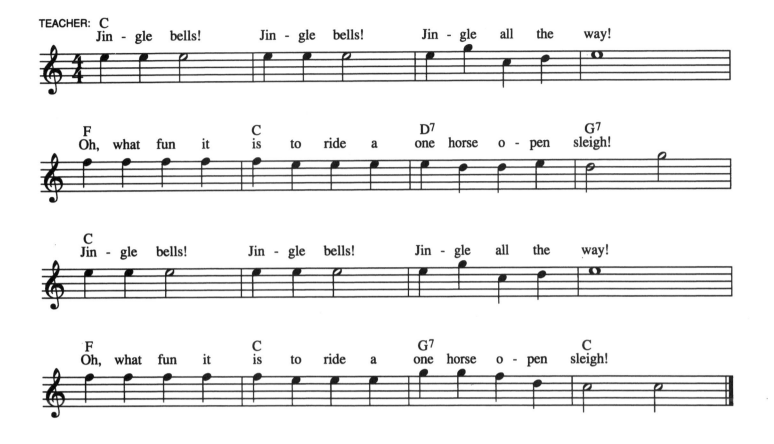

TEACHER: C
Jin - gle bells! Jin - gle bells! Jin - gle all the way!

F   C   D⁷   G⁷
Oh, what fun it is to ride a one horse o - pen sleigh!

C
Jin - gle bells! Jin - gle bells! Jin - gle all the way!

F   C   G⁷   C
Oh, what fun it is to ride a one horse o - pen sleigh!

Many fans affectionately refer to Bruce Springsteen's music as the "soundtrack to their lives" during the 1970s and 1980s. A genuine superstar, "The Boss" is responsible for some of rock's most enduring songs.

Bruce Springsteen

The Third String G

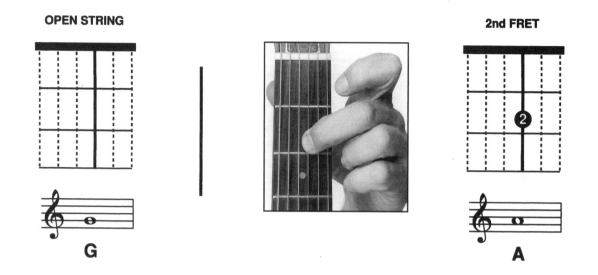

Solos on the Three Highest Strings

Au Clair de la Lune

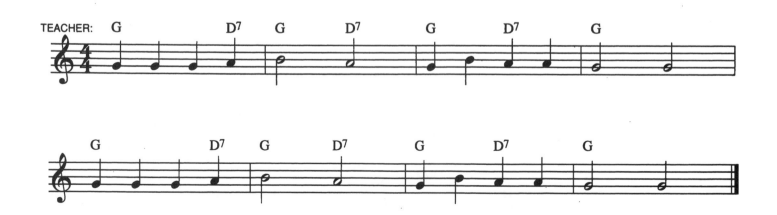

Three-String Rock

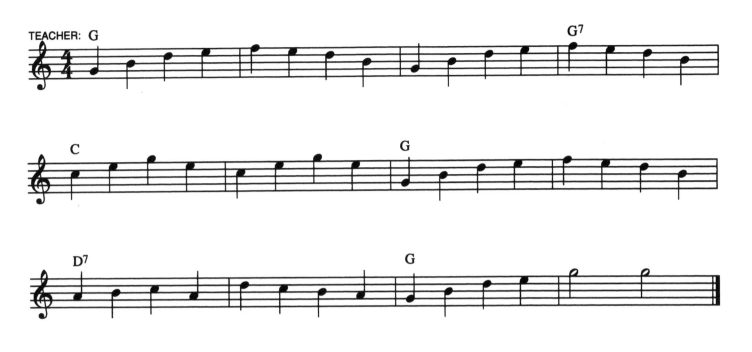

Largo
(from *The New World Symphony*)

Dvořák

Back to the '50s

TEACHER:

Chris Isaak

Chris Isaak's hypnotic sound recalls artists of the past (such as Roy Orbison and Duane Eddy), while remaining original enough to have attracted a following of contemporary rock and pop fans.

Photo: Amy Lehman © 1994

Aura Lee

Elvis Presley recorded this folk song in a modern version called "Love Me Tender."

* The double dots inside the double bars indicate that everything between the double bars must be repeated.

Introducing Chords

A CHORD is a combination of two or more harmonious notes.
All notes except the whole note have a stem going up or down.
When notes are to be struck together as a CHORD, they are
connected by the same stem.

(Not to be played.)

Preliminary Study

Two-note chords on the
open B and E strings.

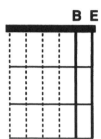

*Play both strings together with one down-stroke.

Three-note chords on the
open G, B, and E strings.

LEARN THE ORDER OF THE STRINGS THOROUGHLY.
PLAY WITH THE WRIST FREE AND RELAXED.
KEEP YOUR EYES ON THE NOTES.

Three-String C Chord

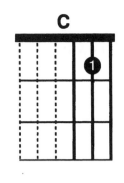
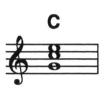

(HOLD C DOWN TO THE END)

Ode to Joy
(Theme from Beethoven's 9th Symphony)

Rock 'n' Rhythm

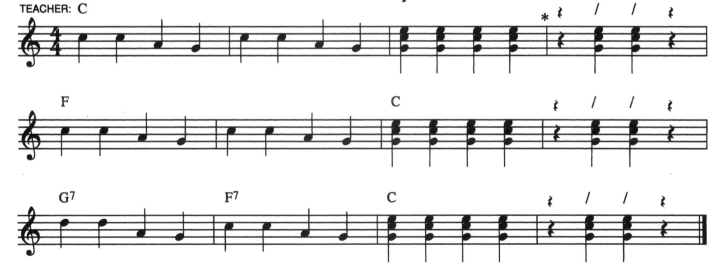

 REST SIGN: indicates silence for one count. For a clearer effect, you may stop the sound of the strings by touching the strings lightly with the "heel" of the right hand.

Three-String G⁷ Chord

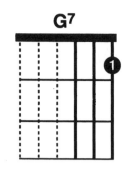

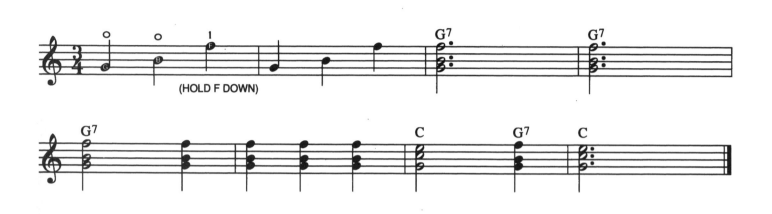

Two-Chord Rock

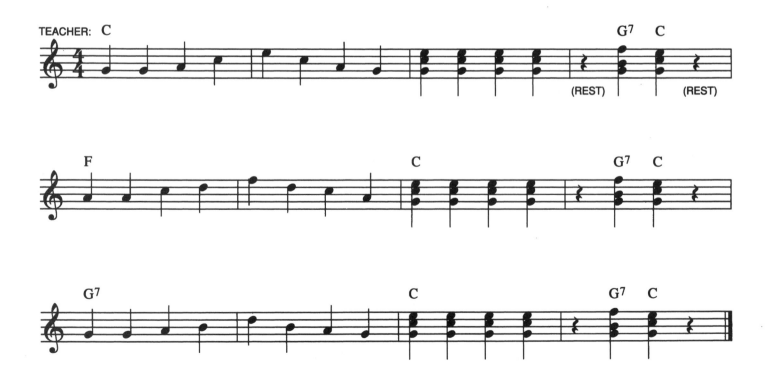

Here is a song for you to sing while you play the accompaniment.

The slanting line below or following a chord symbol (C / / / G7 / / /) means to play the same chord for each line. Repeat the chord until a new chord symbol appears.

Love Somebody

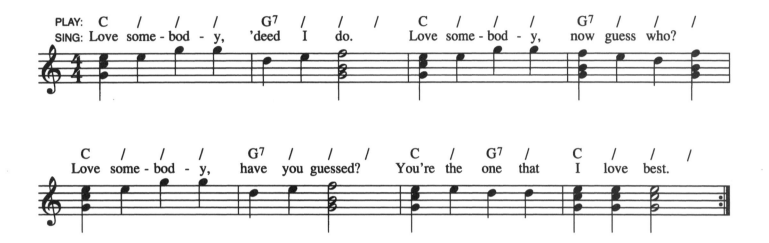

PLAY: C / / / G7 / / / C / / / G7 / / /
SING: Love some - bod - y, 'deed I do. Love some - bod - y, now guess who?

C / / / G7 / / / C / G7 / C / / /
Love some - bod - y, have you guessed? You're the one that I love best.

One of the most controversial figures in 1990s alternative rock, Courtney Love, along with her band Hole, has generated much attention for her raw, emotionally vivid music.

Photo: Amy Lehman © 1995

Courtney Love

Three-String G Chord

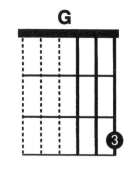

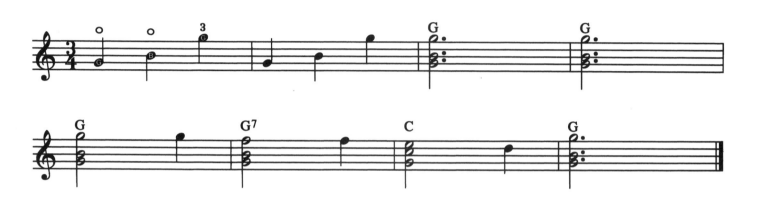

Rockin' with G & C

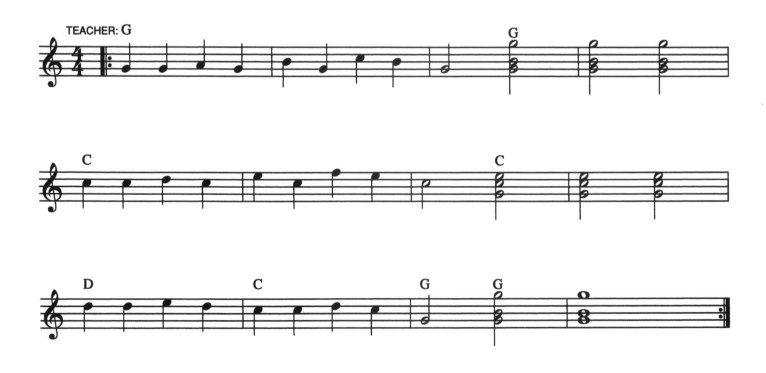

Play this song as a guitar solo by playing the music;
then sing the melody and accompany yourself by playing the chord line.

Down in the Valley

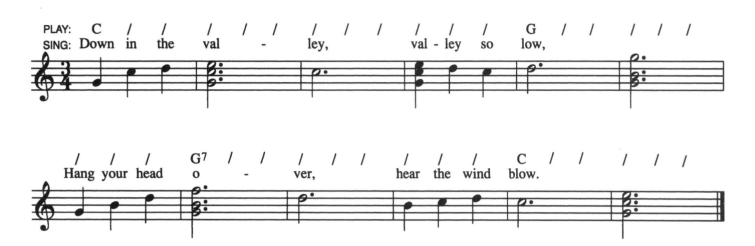

PLAY: C / / / / / / / / / / G / / / / /
SING: Down in the val - ley, val - ley so low,

Hang your head G7 / / / / / / / / C / / / / /
over, hear the wind blow.

Blues legend B.B. King has been making his guitar, "Lucille," sing for many years, and his soulful, heartfelt music has moved generations of fans.

Photo: Cesar Vera

B. B. King

Notes on the Fourth String D

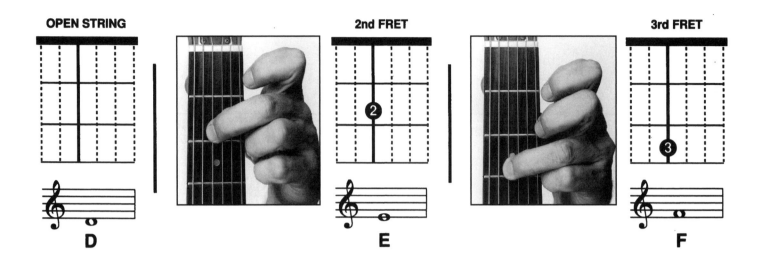

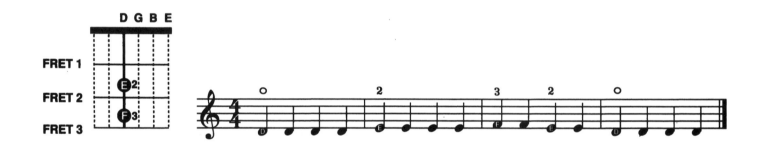

Old MacDonald Had a Farm

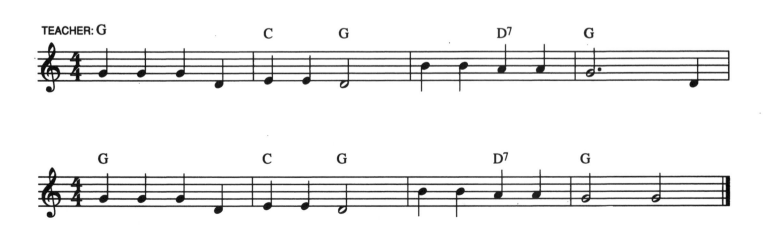

Reuben Reuben

*HOLD SIGN (Fermata or Pause Sign): This sign indicates that the time value of the note is lengthened (approximately twice its usual value).

G Whiz

C means "common time" (the same as 4/4 time).

Bohemian Folk Song

Minor Waltz

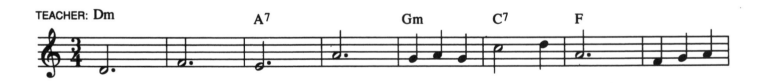

Not all guitar solos are played using one form of the 3-note chords already learned. These songs use various combinations of 2- and 3-note chords.

Good Night, Ladies

Daisy Bell
(A Bicycle Built For Two)

Four-String G & G⁷ Chords

The three-note chords you have learned so far can be expanded to four-note chords that sound fuller and richer. For the G and G7 chords, simply add the open 4th string:

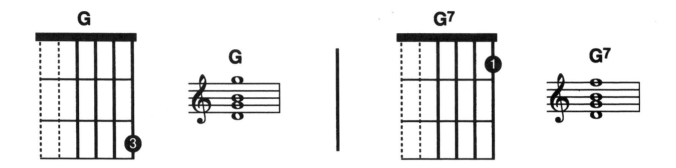

Here is an exercise using expanded four-string versions of the G and G7 chords.

Laughing Polka

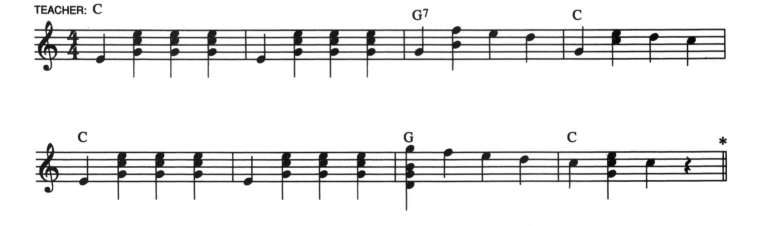

*Two thin lines means the end of a section.

Once a member of the legendary Chess Records house band, Buddy Guy is considered one of the masters of blues guitar playing, and his influence can be heard in most blues-oriented rock music since the 1960s.

Buddy Guy

Photo: Amy Lehman © 1994

The Fifth String A

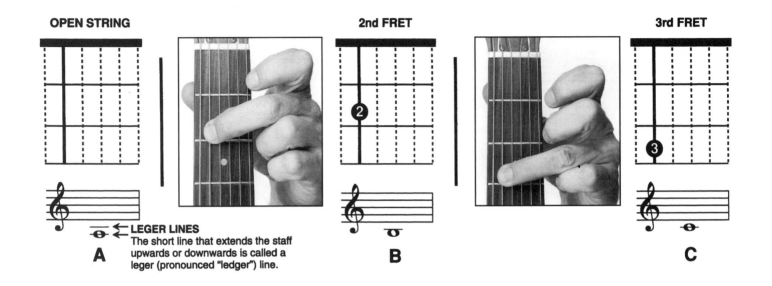

LEGER LINES
The short line that extends the staff upwards or downwards is called a leger (pronounced "ledger") line.

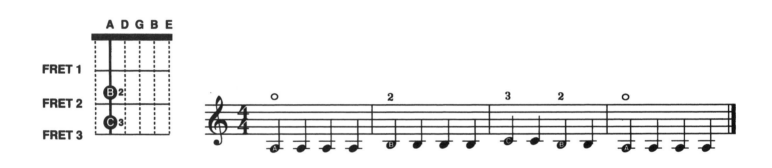

Volga Boatmen

Peter Gray

TEACHER: Am

Texas-born country artist Rosie Flores has had a small but extremely devout following since her days as the guitarist for the all-female cow-punk group, the Screamin' Sirens, in the early-1980s. She has recorded as a solo artist since 1987.

Photo: Amy Lehman © 1995

Rosie Flores

Low-Down Rock

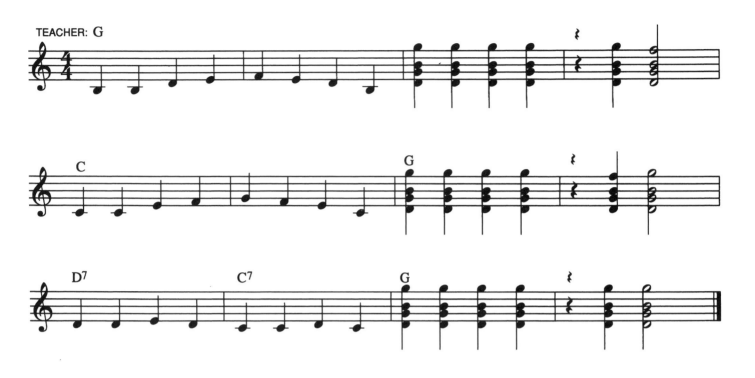

Liebesträum

Boogie Style

John Lee Hooker is considered one of the true fathers of the blues. He has played and recorded through many decades, and his influence is widespread throughout all guitar-based styles of music.

Photo: Institute of Jazz Studies

John Lee Hooker

Introducing High A

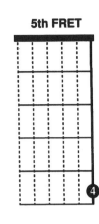

A

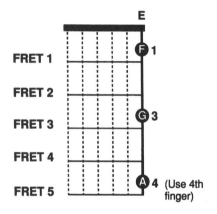

Rockin' in Dorian Mode

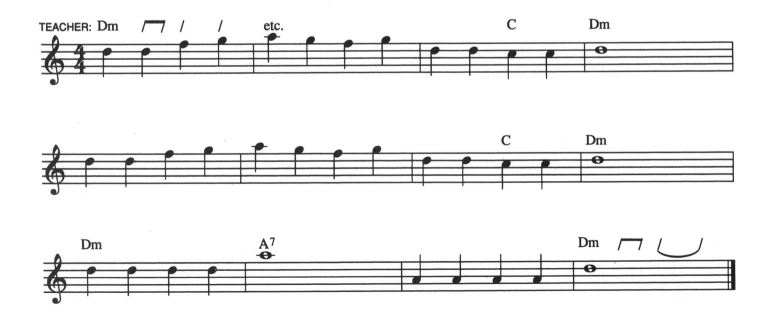

Play *The Riddle Song* in two ways: as a musically complete guitar solo, then as accompaniment while you sing. Strum chords once each beat. May also be played as a duet with your teacher.

The Riddle Song

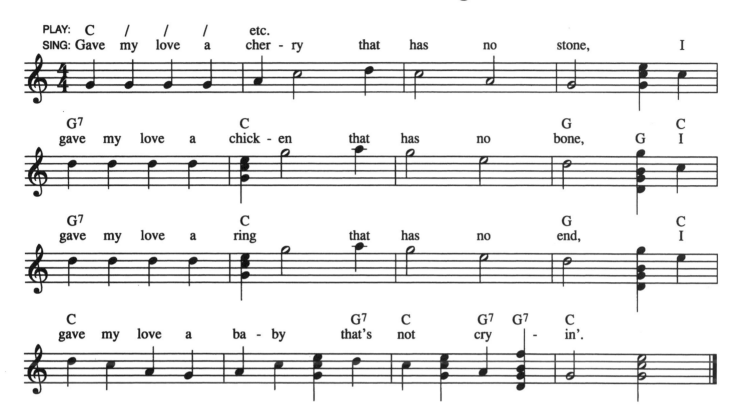

PLAY: C / / / etc.
SING: Gave my love a cher - ry that has no stone, I

gave my love a chick - en that has no bone, G I

gave my love a ring that has no end, I

gave my love a ba - by that's not cry - in'.

Robben Ford has been one of those rare guitarists who can play with proficiency and passion in multiple-styles: rock, blues and jazz. He has worked with artists as diverse as George Harrison and Miles Davis.

Photo: Amy Lehman © 1995

Robben Ford

Incomplete Measures

Not every piece of music begins on the first beat. Music sometimes begins with an incomplete measure, called the UP-BEAT or PICK-UP. If the up-beat is one beat, the last measure will have only three beats in 4/4, or two beats in 3/4.

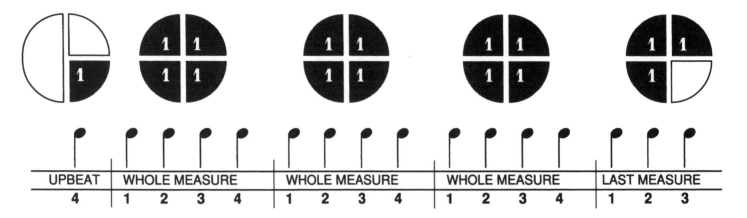

UPBEAT	WHOLE MEASURE	WHOLE MEASURE	WHOLE MEASURE	LAST MEASURE
4	1 2 3 4	1 2 3 4	1 2 3 4	1 2 3

A-tiskit, A-tasket

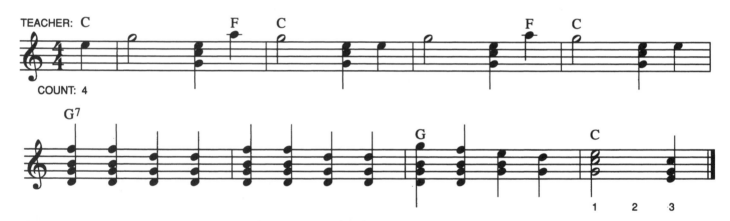

Eric Clapton is a rock icon—his playing has been studied and copied for years. Like other guitar greats of his generation, Clapton was heavily influenced by the blues, which is evident in most of his recordings, ranging from his early work with the Yardbirds and Cream, to his own successful solo work.

Eric Clapton

Photo: Terry O'Neill, Courtesy Reprise Records

The Yellow Rose of Texas

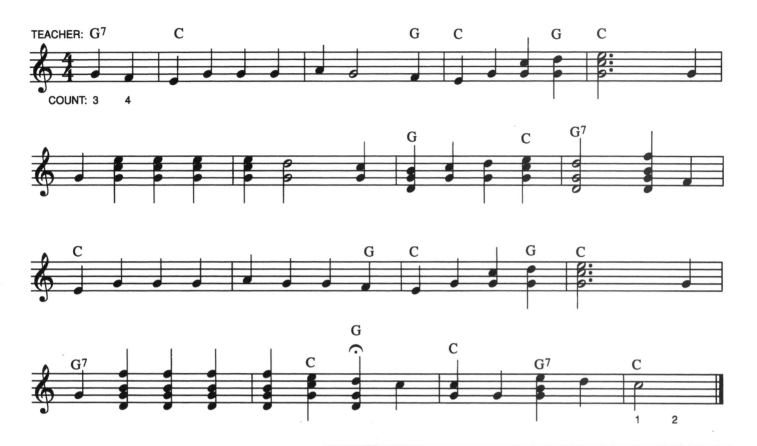

Lyle Lovett has meshed several musical styles together (most notably country, blues and jazz) and come up with a sophisticated, unique sound that has won him a loyal following throughout the 1980s and 1990s.

Photo: Amy Lehman © 1995

Lyle Lovett

The Sixth String E

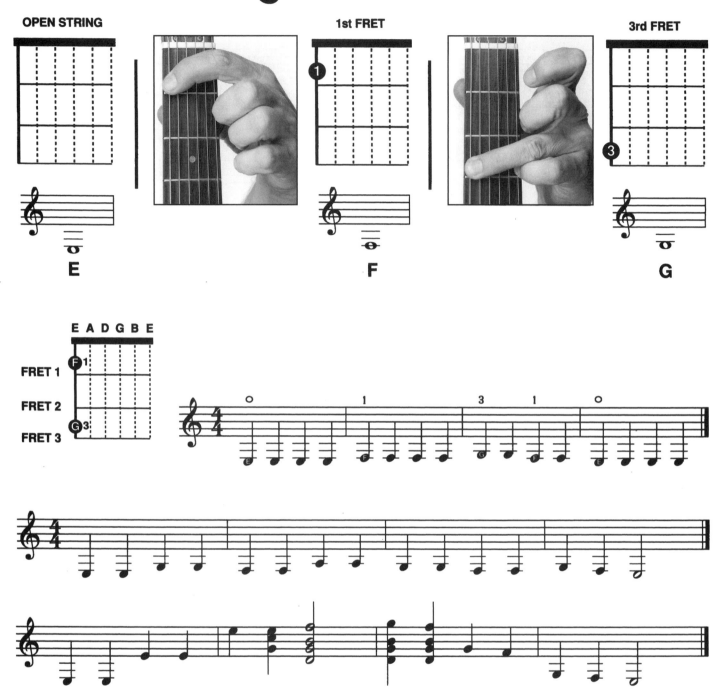

The Natural Scale

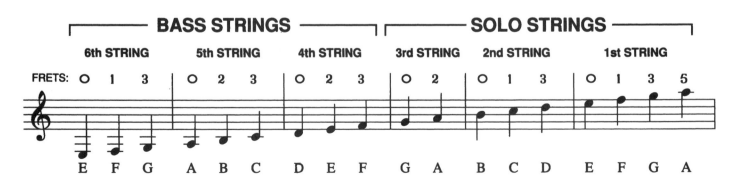

Tempo Signs

The three principal TEMPO SIGNS are
Andante (SLOW), *Moderato* (MODERATELY), *Allegro* (FAST)

Three-Tempo Rock

Play three times: 1st time *Andante*, 2nd time *Moderato*, 3rd time *Allegro*

The Blue Danube Waltz

Plaisir D'amour
(*The Joys of Love*)

G. Martini

Bass-Chord Accompaniment

A popular style of playing chord accompaniments in 4/4 time breaks up the chord into a single note and a smaller chord. Play only the lowest note on the 1st beat (called the bass note), then play the rest of the chord on the 2nd, 3rd and 4th beats. The complete pattern is bass-chord-chord-chord. A variation of this repeats the bass note on the 3rd beat: bass-chord-bass-chord.

Can-Can

Duet*

Allegro

J. Offenbach

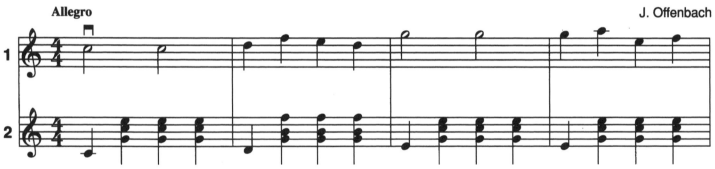

Note: The 2nd part is written in bass-chord-chord-chord style. It can also be played in bass-chord-bass-chord style.

*The 1st and 2nd parts are to be played by the student. The teacher may accompany the student by playing the 2nd part and vice versa. Follow this procedure on subsequent duets unless otherwise indicated.

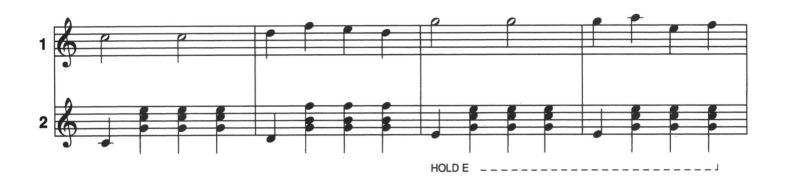

HOLD E ─ ─ ─ ─ ─ ─ ─ ─ ─ ─ ─ ─ ─ ─ ─ ─ ─ ─ ┘

HOLD C ─ ─ ─ ─ ─ ─ ─ ─ ─ ─ ─ ─ ─ ─ ─ ─ ┘

By blending elements of classical music and the blues, Jimmy Page helped shape Led Zepplin's sound, and in the process, became one of the true "guitar-heroes" of the 1970s.

Photo: Robert Night

Jimmy Page

Dynamics

Signs showing how SOFT or LOUD to play are called DYNAMICS.
The principal dynamics are:

𝒑 (Piano) SOFT   𝒎𝒇 (mezzo-forte) MODERATELY LOUD   𝒇 (forte) LOUD   𝒇𝒇 (fortissimo) VERY LOUD

Echo Waltz

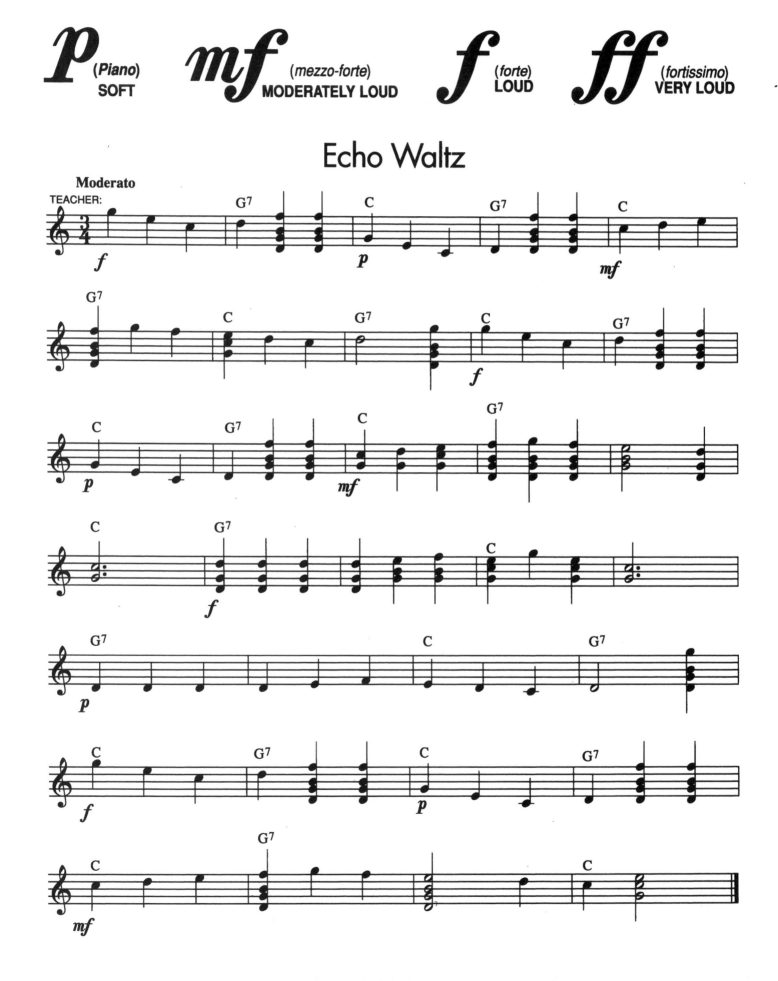

Signs of Silence

QUARTER REST (CROTCHET REST)	= 1 COUNT	
HALF REST (MINIM REST)	= 2 COUNTS	
WHOLE REST (SEMIBREVE REST)	= 4 COUNTS IN 4/4 TIME	
	3 COUNTS IN 3/4 TIME	

The Desert Song
(Study in Counting)

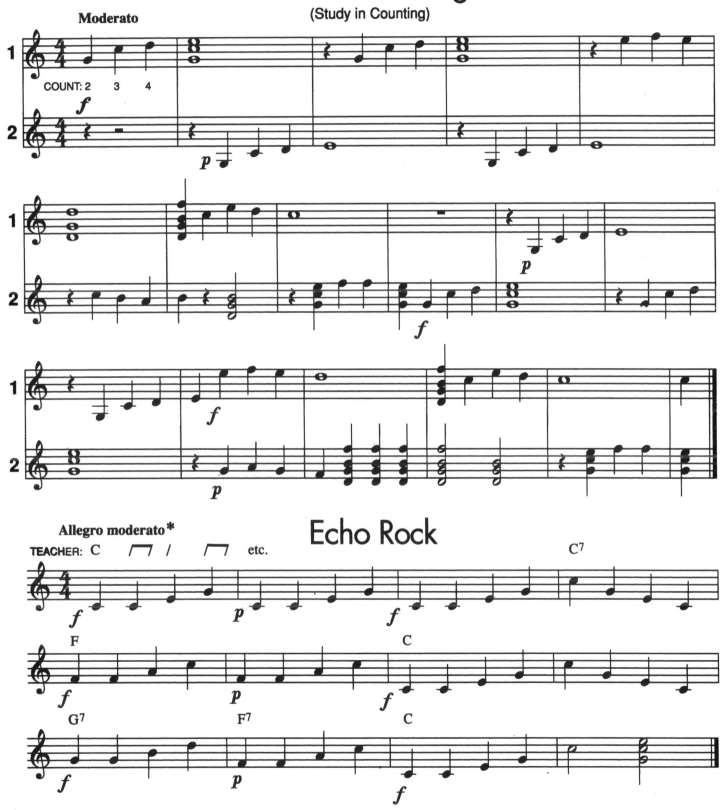

*Two tempo signs may be combined: **Allegro Moderato** means MODERATELY FAST.

Four-String C Chord

The four-string C chord requires placing the 2nd finger on the 2nd fret of the 4th string.

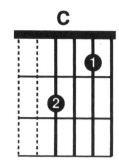

Introducing Ties

A tie is a curved line that connects two or more notes of the same pitch. When two notes are tied, the second one is not played separately. Rather, its value is added to the first note.

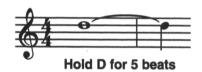

Hold D for 5 beats

When the Saints Go Marching In

Duet or Trio (three players)

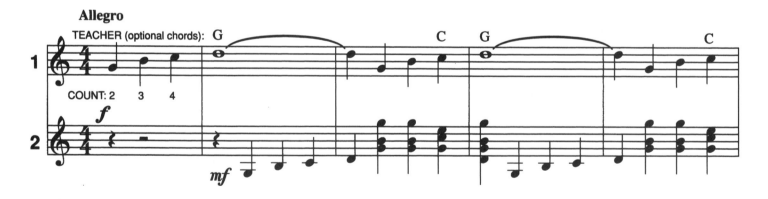

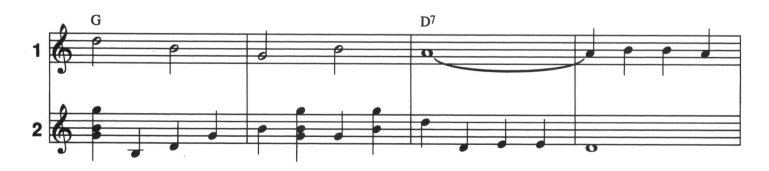

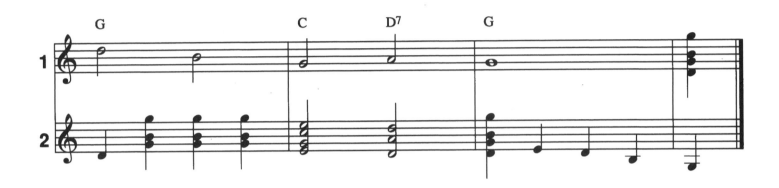

Eddie Van Halen's ground-breaking use of finger-tapping techniques and experimentation with sounds and harmonics have prompted some to call him the best and most exciting guitarist of the 1980s and 1990s.

Photo: Robert Night

Eddie Van Halen

Muddy Waters, *cited by many as the inventor of "electric blues," was one of the dominant figures in post-war blues. Although criticized by some for his use of amplification, he ultimately opened the door to a new generation of blues enthusiasts.*

Photo: Institute of Jazz Studies

Muddy Waters

More Bass-Chord Accompaniments

When a piece is in 3/4 time, a popular style of chord accompaniment is bass-chord-chord. The bass note is the note that names the chord (C for the C chord, G for G or G7 chords). Usually the bass note is also the lowest note in the chord. First play the bass note alone, then the rest of the chord on the 2nd and 3rd beats.

If a chord is repeated for two or more measures, an *alternate* bass note (another note in the chord) is used to get a greater variety of sound.

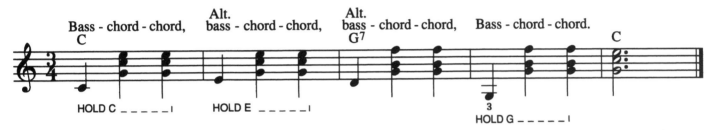

Whether fronting the 1980s supergroup The Police or exploring his own brand of jazz-infused pop music as a solo artist, *Sting* has always been an adventurous, highly-innovative artist. Although primarily known as a bass player, he often plays guitar on his albums and in concert, most notably the acoustic solo on his 1988 hit single "Fragile."

Photo: Amy Lehman © 1994

Sting

Chiapanecas

Mexican Handclapping Song

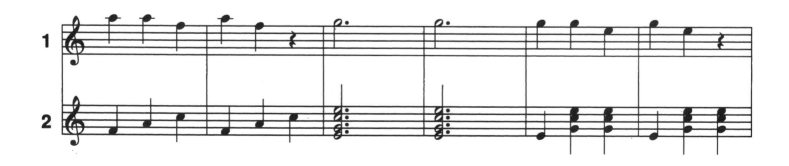

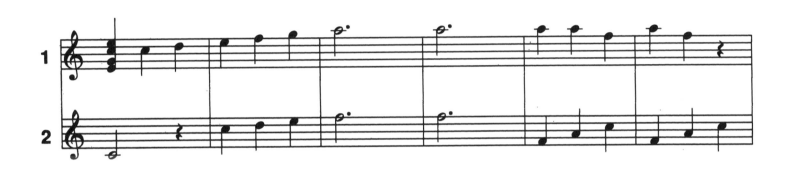

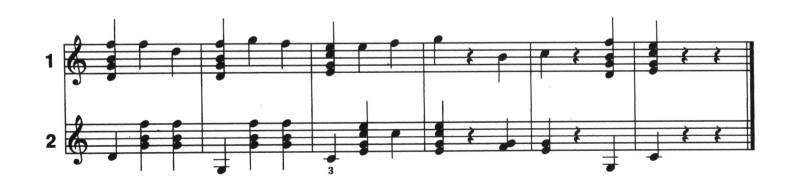

Eighth Notes (Quavers)

Eighth notes are the black notes with a flag added to the stem ♪ or ♭ .

Two or more eighth notes are written ⌐⌐ or ♫ .

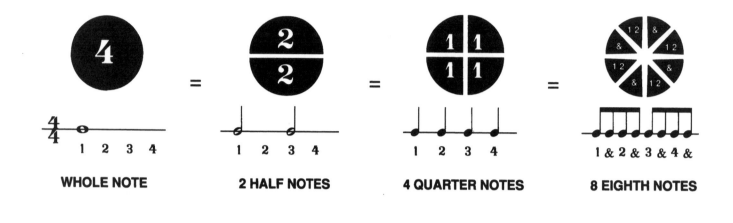

USE ALTERNATING
DOWNSTROKES ⊓
AND UPSTROKES V
ON EIGHTH NOTES.

COUNT: 1 & 2 & 3 & 4 &   1 & 2 & 3 & 4 &

Eighth-Note Bounce

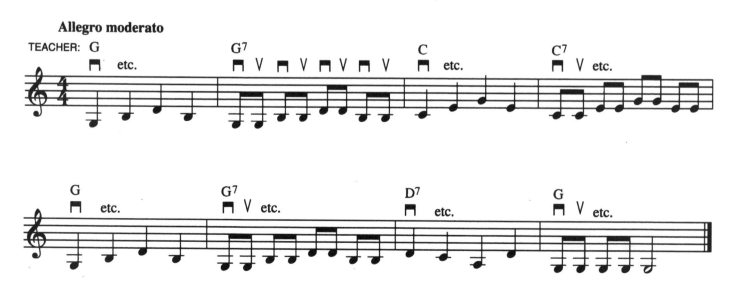

Walkin' Bass Rock

Allegro moderato

TEACHER: G

George Harrison earned his nickname of "the quiet Beatle" in the early 1960s for his easygoing attitude, but it also applies to his attitude toward playing the guitar. Never flashy unless the song calls for it, Harrison's trademark sound incorporates blues riffs with pure pop hooks.

Photo: Terry O'Neill © 1980

George Harrison with Paul McCartney

Pachelbel's Canon

Play as a Round. 1st player plays as usual. 2nd player begins when 1st player gets to [A] .

Slow and stately

Johann Pachelbel

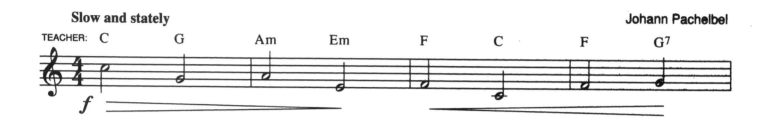

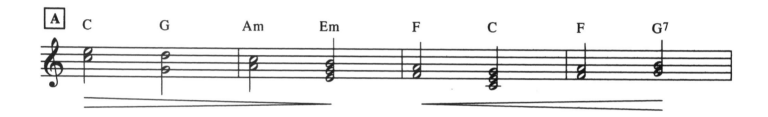

The sign ―――――― or the word *crescendo,* means GROW GRADUALLY LOUDER.

The sign ―――――― or the word *diminuendo,* means GROW GRADUALLY SOFTER.

The Who took a larger-than-life approach to rock performance, perhaps inspired by guitarist Pete Townshend's compositions, which were as theatrical as they were powerful. Included among these was rock's first opera, *Tommy,* released in 1969.

Photo: Ethan Russel, Courtesy MCA

The Who

Sharps ♯, Flats ♭ and Naturals ♮

The distance from one fret to the next fret, up or down
is a HALF STEP. TWO half steps make a WHOLE STEP.

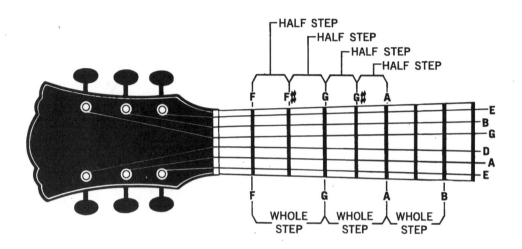

HALF STEPS • NO FRET BETWEEN

WHOLE STEPS • ONE FRET BETWEEN

 SHARPS RAISE the note a half step. Play the next fret higher.

 FLATS LOWER the note a half step. If the note is fingered, play next fret lower. If the note is open, play the 4th fret of the next lower string except if that string is G (3rd string), then play the 3rd fret.

 NATURALS CANCEL a previous sharp or flat.

The Chromatic Scale

The CHROMATIC SCALE is formed exclusively of HALF STEPS.
The ascending chromatic scale uses SHARPS (♯). The descending chromatic scale uses FLATS (♭).

Chromatic Rock

Allegro moderato

My Melancholy Baby

Slowly

G. Norton and E. Burnett

* When a sharped or flatted note appears more than once in the same measure, it is still played sharp or flat unless cancelled by a natural.

Four-String D⁷ Chord

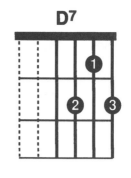

Four-Beat Blues

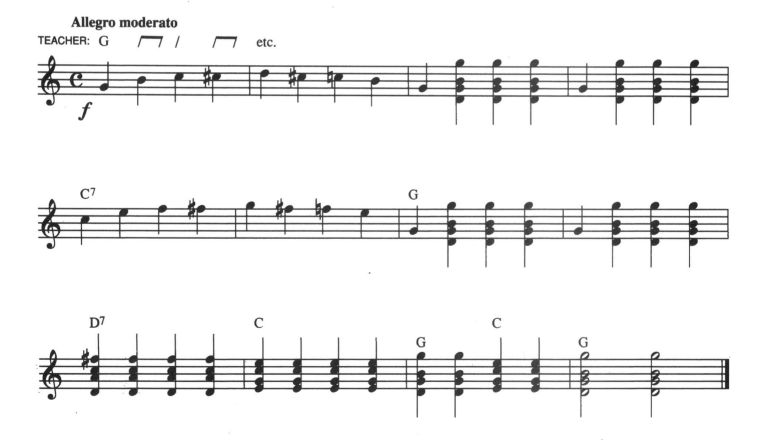

Amazing Grace

Andante

*The 2nd F in the measure is also sharp. Sharps or flats affect every note on the same line or space in the measure in which they appear.

Thought to be the most brilliant soloist of his time, **Charlie Christian** was among the first jazz guitarists to amplify his instrument. Consequently, his guitar was able to equal and even surpass the volume and power of wind instruments.

Photo: Institute of Jazz Studies

Charlie Christian

Rockin' the Bach

Adapted from a Bach Minuet

Buffalo Gals

Play *Buffalo Gals* in two ways—as a musically complete guitar solo, then as accompaniment while you sing. Strum chords once each beat.

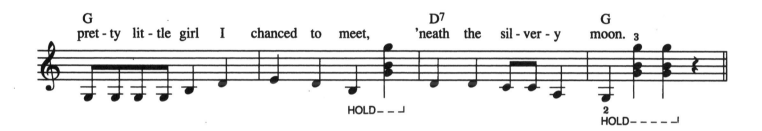

The Major Scale

A scale is a succession of eight tones in alphabetical order.
All major scales are built in the same form.

**WHOLE STEP,   WHOLE STEP,   HALF STEP,
WHOLE STEP,   WHOLE STEP,   WHOLE STEP,   HALF STEP**

THE OCTAVE NOTE
This scale has eight notes. The highest note, having the same letter-name as the first note is called the Octave note.

C MAJOR SCALE

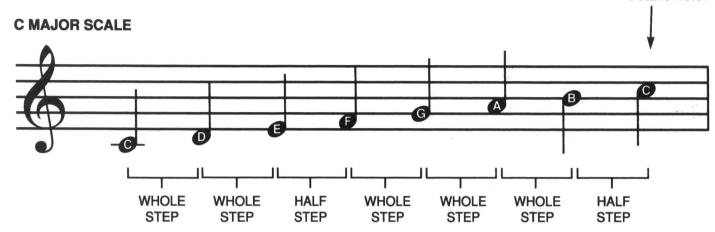

It is easier to visualize whole steps and half steps on a piano keyboard. Notice there are whole steps between every natural note except E-F, and B-C.

WHOLE STEPS · ONE KEY BETWEEN

HALF STEPS · NO KEY BETWEEN

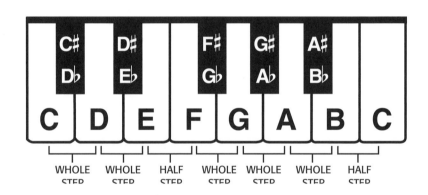

A MAJOR SCALE may be built starting on ANY NOTE, natural, sharp or flat.
Using this pattern, write a MAJOR SCALE, starting on G:

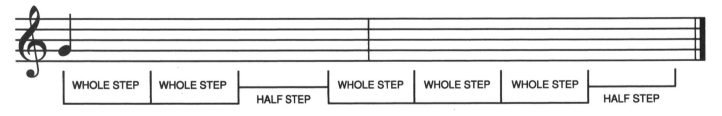

Write a MAJOR SCALE, starting on F:

CHECK: Are the notes in alphabetical order?

Key Signatures

The Key of C Major

A piece based on the C MAJOR SCALE is in the KEY OF C MAJOR. Since there are no sharps or flats in the C scale, any sharps or flats occurring in a piece in the KEY OF C MAJOR are called ACCIDENTALS.

The Key of G Major

A piece based on the G MAJOR SCALE is in the KEY OF G MAJOR. Since F is sharp in the G scale, every F will be sharp in the key of G major. Instead of making all the F's sharp in the piece, the sharp is indicated at the beginning, in the KEY SIGNATURE. Sharps or flats shown in the KEY SIGNATURE are effective throughout the piece.

Key Signature
One Sharp (F♯)

The Key of F Major

A piece based on the F MAJOR SCALE is in the KEY OF F MAJOR.

Key Signature
One Flat (B♭)

If sharps, flats or naturals not shown in the key signature occur in the piece, they are called ACCIDENTALS. ACCIDENTALS are effective only for the measures in which they appear.

The three scales shown above should be practiced every day. Students who do this will have little difficulty playing selections written in C MAJOR, G MAJOR and F MAJOR.

Eighth Rests

This is an EIGHTH REST.
It means REST for the value of an EIGHTH NOTE.

When eighth notes appear singly, they look like this: ♪ or ♭

Single eighth notes are often used with eighth rests: ♪ ♪

Count: "one &"
or: "two - 8ths"

Clap (or tap) the following rhythm:

When playing a fingered note, the sound is cut off by releasing the pressure of the finger on the string. When playing an open note, the sound is cut off by touching the string with either a left hand finger or the "heel" of the right hand.

Eighth rests may also appear on downbeats. This creates no unusual problem if the student MARKS THE DOWNBEAT BY TAPPING THE FOOT or mentally counting.

Bill Bailey

H. Cannon

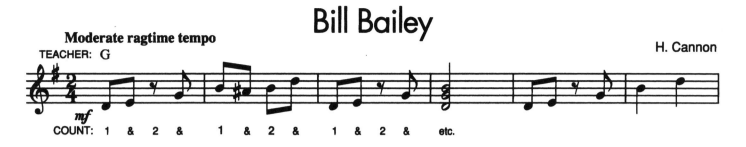

La Bamba

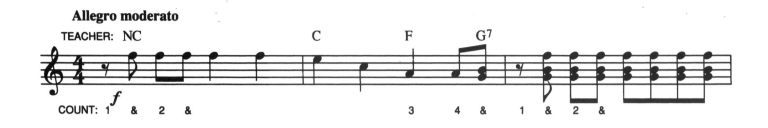

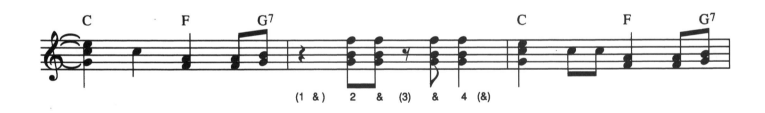

Introducing Dotted Quarter (Dotted Crotchet) Notes

A DOT INCREASES THE LENGTH OF A NOTE BY ONE-HALF!

Preparatory Drill

COUNT: 1 & 2 & 3 & 4 &   1 & 2 & 3 & 4 &   1 & 2 & 3 & 4 &

The only difference in the following two measures and those directly above them is the way they are written. They should sound the SAME.

COUNT: 1 & 2 & 3 & 4 &   1 & 2 & 3 & 4 &

British guitarist *Allan Holdsworth* has pushed the boundaries of guitar playing in the late 20th century, both with the progressive rock band UK, as well as with his own solo career. Eddie Van Halen is among his many fans.

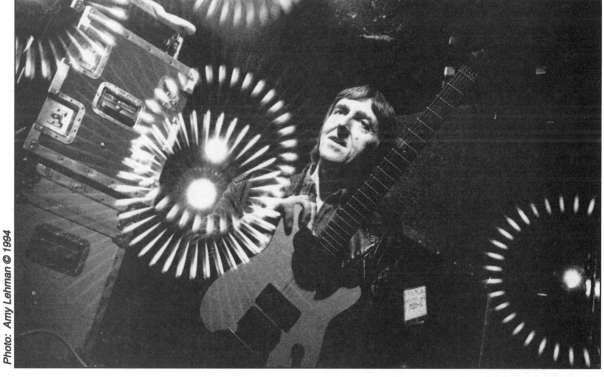

Photo: Amy Lehman © 1994

Allan Holdsworth

Auld Lang Syne

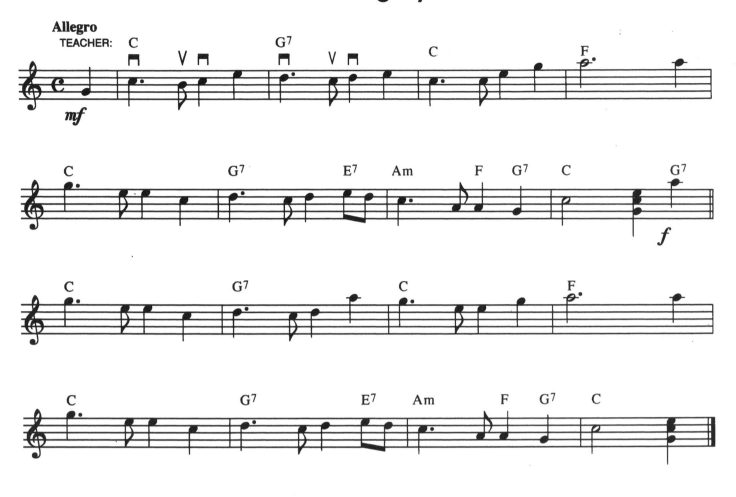

Hava Nagila

Israeli Folk Song

* > = Accent mark—play the note a little louder.

Key of C Major

C MAJOR SCALE

Three Chords in C

In the diagrams above and throughout this book the black dots show where to place the fingers and the number inside the dot indicates which finger to use. No dot means open string; the string played but not fingered. The string with the dotted line means that string is not to be played.

USE DOWN-STROKES ONLY

Accompaniment in C Major

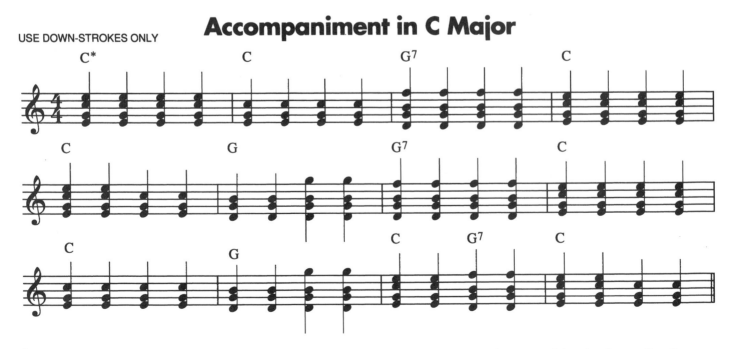

*When introduced, chord names are written above the chords so the student may learn the notes of the chord as well as its name.

The C major scale can be extended to a full two octaves by adding high A, high B and high C.

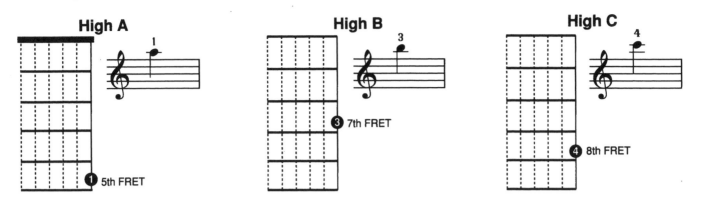

The ascending two-octave C major scale.

SHIFT THE HAND UP THE NECK

The descending two-octave C major scale.

SHIFT DOWN THE NECK

Practice these scales every day. Make every effort to play the sections marked with a [   ] as smoothly as possible.

Rakes of Mallow

Allegro

Irish Fiddle Tune

74

The F minor is a new chord that requires you to put down your 1st finger across three strings. Press hard near (but not on) the 1st fret.

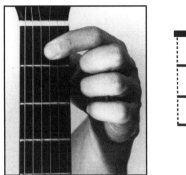
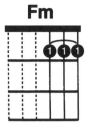

Home on the Range

The melody may be sung or played.

American Cowboy Song

Oh, give me a home where the buf - fa - lo roam, where the

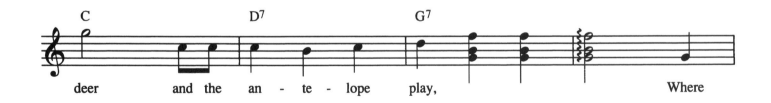

deer and the an - te - lope play, Where

sel - dom is heard a dis - cour - ag - ing word and the

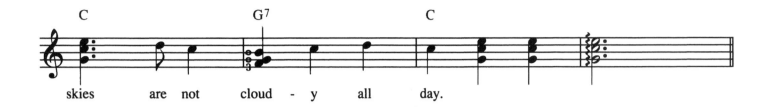

skies   are   not   cloud - y   all   day.

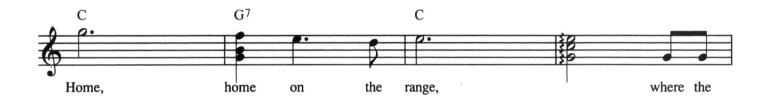

Home,   home   on   the   range,   where the

deer   and   the   an - te - lope   play,   Where

sel - dom   is   heard   a dis - cour - ag - ing   word   and the

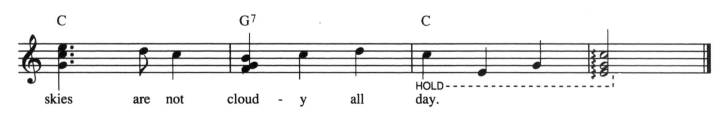

skies   are   not   cloud - y   all   day.

HOLD -

* A wavy line in front of a chord ⦃ means to run the pick across the strings more slowly to obtain a rippling, harp-like sound. The technical name for this effect is the Italian word "arpeggiando," usually abbreviated "arp."

Tunes that Teach Technic No. 1

Variations on
Little Brown Jug

For developing technic in repeated notes.

Variations on
Jim Crack Corn

Combining scale passages and chords.

* The symbol 𝄵 means "cut time," that is, the time value is cut in half; the half notes receive 1 beat, the quarter notes receive 1/2 beat, etc.

Bass Solos with Chord Accompaniment

When bass solos are played with chord accompaniment, the solo part is written with the stems descending, the chords with the stems ascending.

The bass solo begins on the first beat and is held for three beats. The quarter rest shows that the chord accompaniment begins on the 2nd beat.

Example:

Meet Me In St. Louis, Louis

A.B. Sterling,
Kerry Mills

Key of G Major

The key signature of one sharp indicates the key of G major.
All F's are played as F♯ unless otherwise indicated by a natural sign.

G MAJOR SCALE

The Three Principal Chords in G

The three principal (most commonly used) chords in any key are built on the first, fourth and
fifth notes of the scale. The chord built on the fifth note usually adds a seventh tone to it.
The chords are known as 1, 4, 5(7) chords and are notated by Roman numerals: I, IV, V7.
The three principal chords in the key of G are G, C and D7.

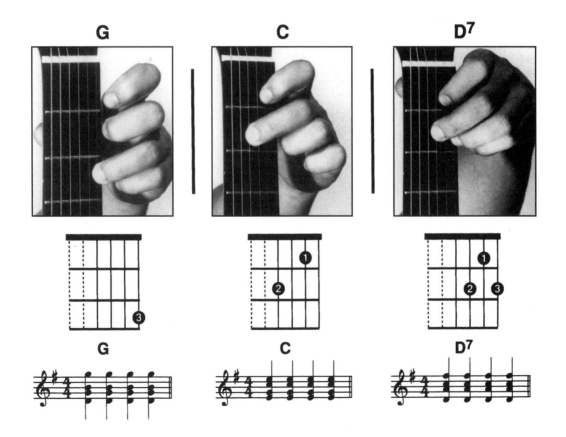

On the next song, first learn the melody. It's in the key of G and makes use of many repeated notes. Then have your teacher or a friend play the melody while you strum the chords, four to each measure.

Tiritomba

Italian Folk Song

The Old Chisholm Trail
(Duet)

Student to learn both parts. Then play as a duet with your teacher or a friend.
Finally, sing the melody (top staff) while playing the accompaniment (bottom staff).

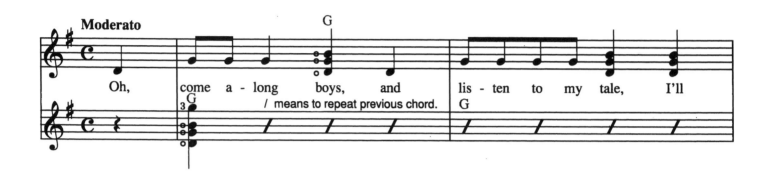

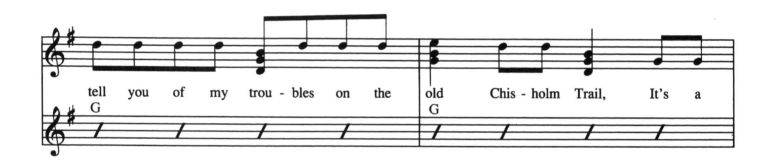

*Remember: F is played ♯ in the key of G.

Ain't Gonna Rain

(Duet)

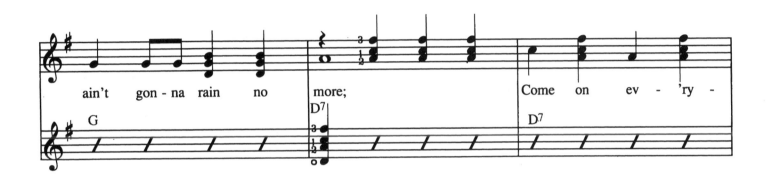

This Land Is Your Land
(Duet)

Student to learn both parts.

Woody Guthrie

This land is your land,___ this land is my land ___

___ From Cal - i - for - nia___ to the New York is - land,___

___ From the red - wood for - est___ to the Gulf Stream wa - ters,___

*One of the living legends of rock music, **Bob Dylan** incorporates many styles in his guitar playing. After starting with traditional folk and blues, and then "going electric" in 1965, he continues to explore new musical sounds. His contemporary musical work still receives great critical acclaim.*

Photo: Frank Micelotta, Courtesy of Sony

Bob Dylan

Tunes that Teach Technic No. 2

Margarita
(Study in 3rds)

Introducing D and B played together*

March tempo

TEACHER: G

G   *

C   G   D⁷   G

Shortnin' Bread
(For developing fluency in skips)

Moderato

TEACHER: G

Red River Valley
(Duet)

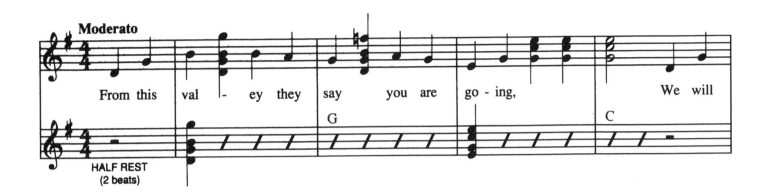

From this val - ey they say you are go - ing,   We will

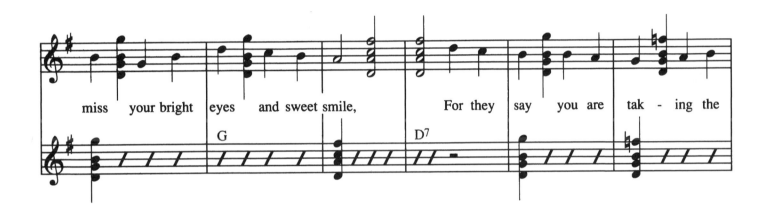

miss your bright eyes and sweet smile,   For they say you are tak - ing the

sun - shine,   That bright - ens our path - way a - while.

God Save the Queen

(Duet)

One of the true Chicago bluesmen to come into prominence during the 1960s, **Magic Sam** was an attraction at many rock performances, where he helped introduce the blues to a new generation of fans. Tragically, he died at the age of 32, before his career had a chance to truly take off.

Photo: Institute of Jazz Studies

Magic Sam

Syncopation

Syncopation is the name given to a musical effect in which a note is anticipated, that is, played before its expected beat. For example, this rhythm is not syncopated—each quarter note falls in the expected place, *on* the beat.

The following example uses syncopation. The 3rd quarter note is played on the "and" of the 2nd beat, rather than its expected place on the 3rd beat. For best results, count carefully and accent > (play a little louder) all syncopated notes.

The following syncopations occur in the next tune you will learn. Practice them carefully before attempting "The Entertainer" (page 88).

The first music to make extensive use of syncopation was called ragtime. It became very popular about a hundred years ago. This ragtime composition was used as the main theme for the movie, "The Sting."

The Entertainer
(Duet)

Student to learn both parts.

Scott Joplin

89

Key of A Minor

For every major key, there is a minor key with the same signature called the RELATIVE MINOR KEY. The keys of A minor and C major are relative keys because they have the same key signature (no sharps, no flats). The relative minor scale is built on the 6th tone of the major scale. Chords are built on the harmonic minor scale which has its 7th step augmented (raised a half step).

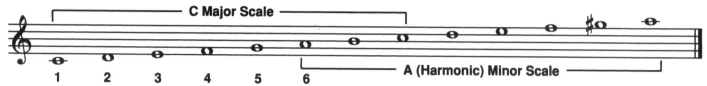

The two-octave A (harmonic) minor scale.

The Three Principal Chords in the Key of A Minor

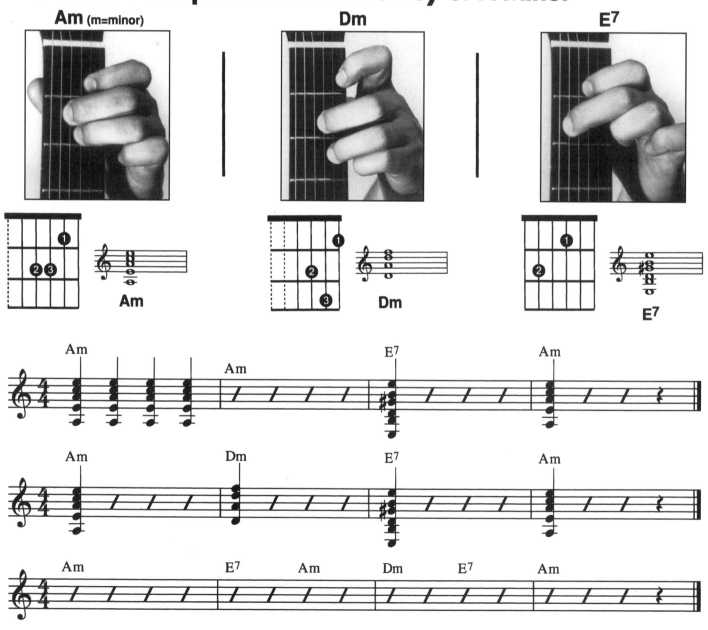

Waves of the Danube

This melody by Romanian composer Ion Ivanovici is frequently played at anniversary celebrations.

*Play from the beginning to the ⊕; then skip directly to the coda (the last two measures).

Bass-Chord Accompaniment: Key of C

Chord Accompaniment is considerably improved by replacing the first chord of each measure with a bass note. The simplest bass note is the root (the letter-name) of the chord. The three principal chords in the key of C are C, F and G7.

With the C (I) chord, play the bass note C.

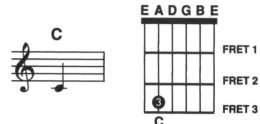

With the F (IV) chord, play the bass note F.

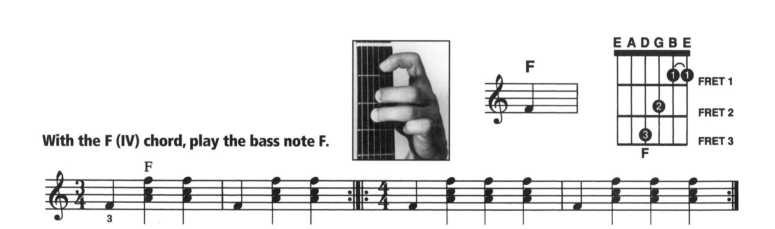

With the G or G7 (V7) chord, play the bass note G.

*On certain occasions, it is preferable to use the thumb for bass notes on the low E string when followed by a chord. Try both fingerings and use the one that is easier for you.

Bass–Chord–Chord–Chord

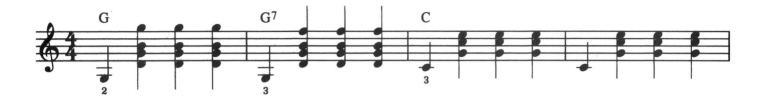

T-Bone Walker *helped turn the electric guitar from a novelty to a blues standard. Incorporating more sophisticated jazz into his music, he expanded the blues's breadth and appeal. His flamboyant performing style also set the precedent for rockers like Chuck Berry and Jimi Hendrix.*

Photo: Institute of Jazz Studies

T-Bone Walker

The Yellow Rose of Texas

(Duet)

Moderato

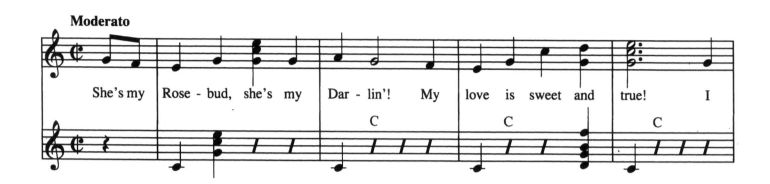

She's my Rose - bud, she's my Dar - lin'! My love is sweet and true! I

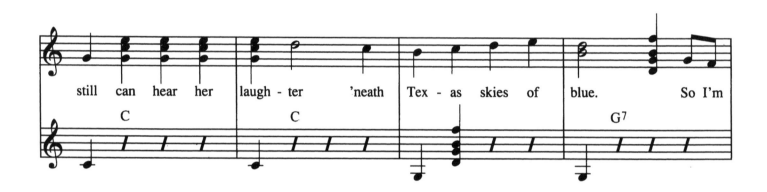

still can hear her laugh - ter 'neath Tex - as skies of blue. So I'm

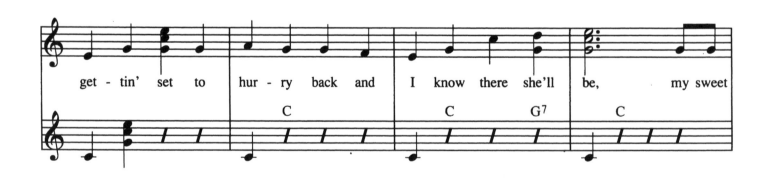

get - tin' set to hur - ry back and I know there she'll be, my sweet

Yel - low Rose of Tex - as there a - wait - in' faith - ful - ly.

$\frac{6}{8}$ Time

The time signature $\frac{6}{8}$ = six beats in each measure
= a beat on an eighth note

Count: 1 2 3 4 5 6

Note and rest values in $\frac{6}{8}$

1 2 3 4 5 6 1 2 3 4 5 6 1 2 3 4 5 6 1 2 3 4 5 6 1 2 3 4 5 6

Drink to Me Only with Thine Eyes

The Eyes of Texas

For He's a Jolly Good Fellow

*Go back to the sign 𝄋
and play to the *Fine*.

Funiculi, Funicula

The Irish Washerwoman

Irish Folk Tune

*One of the most popular bands to emerge during the mid-1990s, hailing from Ireland, the Cranberries play compelling pop-tunes upon which lead-singer **Delores O'Riordan's** hypnotic vocals soar.*

Bass-Chord Accompaniment: Key of G

The three principal chords in the key of G are G, C, D7:

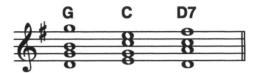

THE THREE PRINCIPAL CHORDS WITH THE ROOT* BASS.

Bass–Chord–Chord–Chord

Bass–Chord–Bass–Chord

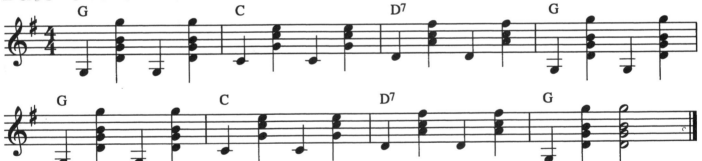

Bass–Chord Variation

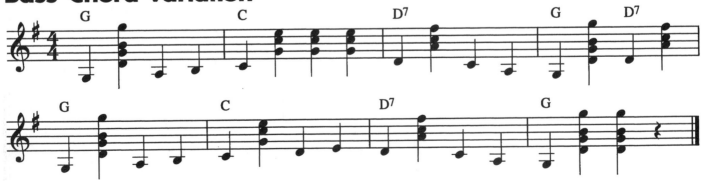

*The root of a chord is the note that names it. For example, the root of a G chord is the note G; the root of a D7 chord is D and so on.

Oh! Susanna

(Duet)

Stephen Foster

The Key of D Major

The key signature of two sharps indicates the key of D major. All F's are played as F# and all C's are played as C# unless otherwise indicated by a natural sign. To play the two-octave D major scale, you'll need two new notes on the 1st string, high C# (1st string, 9th fret) and high D (1st string, 10th fret).

When learning the two-octave D major scale below, follow the fingering carefully. Like all scales, this one should be practiced daily.

The Three Principal Chords in D with Bass Notes

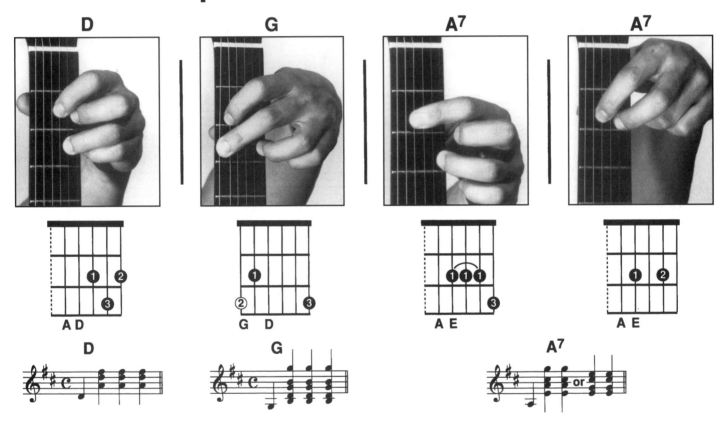

Accompaniment in D Major

Two Etudes in D

The student should learn both the melody and the accompanying chords of this Christmas favorite.

Joy to the World

Marines Hymn
(Duet)

The Dotted 8th & 16th Note Rhythm

Like 8th notes, dotted 8ths and 16ths are played two to each beat. But unlike 8th notes (which are played evenly) dotted 8ths and 16ths are played unevenly: long, short, long, short.
Compare the following:

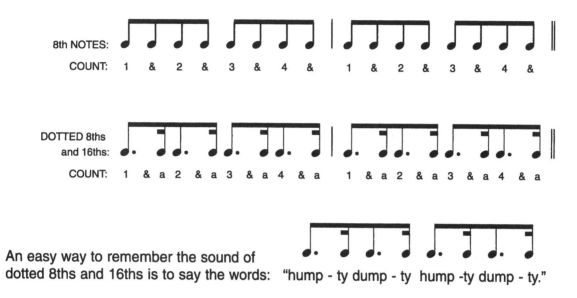

An easy way to remember the sound of dotted 8ths and 16ths is to say the words: "hump - ty dump - ty hump -ty dump - ty."

The dotted 8th and 16th note rhythm is very common in all kinds of music, but especially classical, folk, country, and blues. Here are examples of each to practice.

Toreador Song (from *Carmen*)

Geo. Bizet

104

Student to play melody and chords.

Straight Jig

Irsh Folk Tune

Moderato

TEACHER: Am

*E sharp is the same as F natural (1st string, 1st fret).

Student to play melody and chords.

Boogie Blues

Moderato

TEACHER: G

The dotted 8th and 16th note rhythm can be combined with bass-chord style to create a type of accompaniment called the "shuffle beat." Keep in mind the "hump-ty dump-ty" rhythm of the accompaniment and use down- and up-picking to accomplish it.

Careless Love
(Duet)

Traditional Blues

* ⅀. means to repeat previous measure.

Alternating Bass Notes

An alternating bass note is any note except the root of the chord (usually the 5th). Alternate bass notes are used to enrich the accompaniment when the harmony remains the same for several consecutive measures.

The accompaniment is good:

But this is better:

Alternating Bass Notes in the Key of C

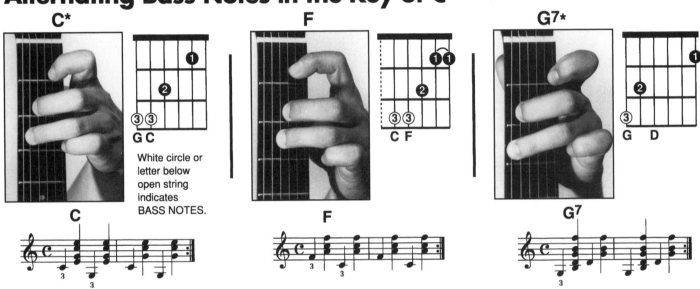

Accompaniment in C Major

*Here are complete forms of the C and G7 chords. If the stretches can be handled, their use is preferred when playing accompaniment. Finger the complete chord at the beginning of the measure and hold it until the chord changes.

I Ride an Old Paint*
(Duet)

*A paint is a horse with a smear of color.

**Pull off means: Do not pick the 2nd note. Pull the 2nd finger off the string so that the open G note sounds.

Alternating Bass Notes in the Key of G

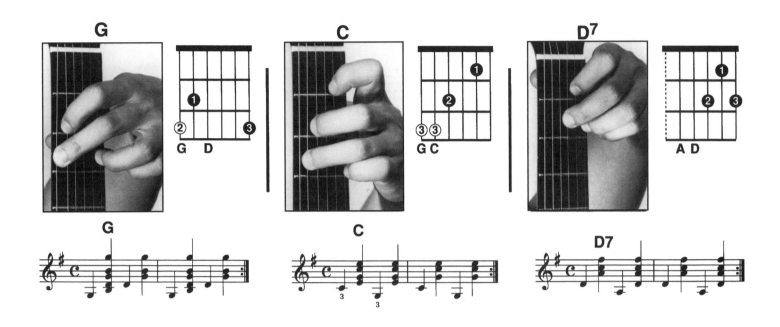

Accompaniment in G Major

Hand Me Down My Walking Cane
(Duet)

Introducing Triplets

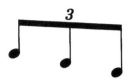

When three notes are grouped together with the figure "3" above or below the notes, the group is called a TRIPLET. The three notes then have the same value as is ordinarily given to two of the notes. In 3/4 or 4/4 times, two eighth notes get one count, so an eighth note TRIPLET will also get one count.

In the following exercise play the three notes of each triplet on one count.

Triumphal March (from *Aida*)

Giuseppe Verdi

Maestoso
(Majestically)

Fine

D.C. al Fine*

**D.C.* means go back to the beginning. *D.C. al Fine* means go back to the beginning and play to the end (*Fine*).

Beautiful Dreamer

Stephen Foster

Sweet Genevieve

SING: Oh, Gen-e-vieve, sweet Gen-e-vieve, The days may come, the days may go, But still the hands of mem-'ry weave the bliss-ful dreams of long a-go.

*Since the 1960s, **Neil Young** has been a rock 'n' roll chameleon, always exploring new styles, often incorporating obscure styles years before they became popular. He is one of popular music's greatest pioneers.*

Key of E Minor

E minor and G Major are relative keys, they both have the key signature of one sharp (F#.) Like the A minor scale, the E minor scale is built on the 6th tone of the relative (G) major.

The two-octave E harmonic minor scale.

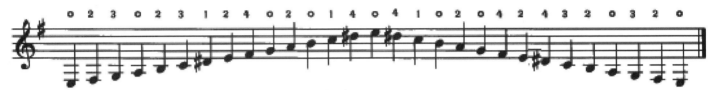

The Three Principal Chords in the Key of E Minor

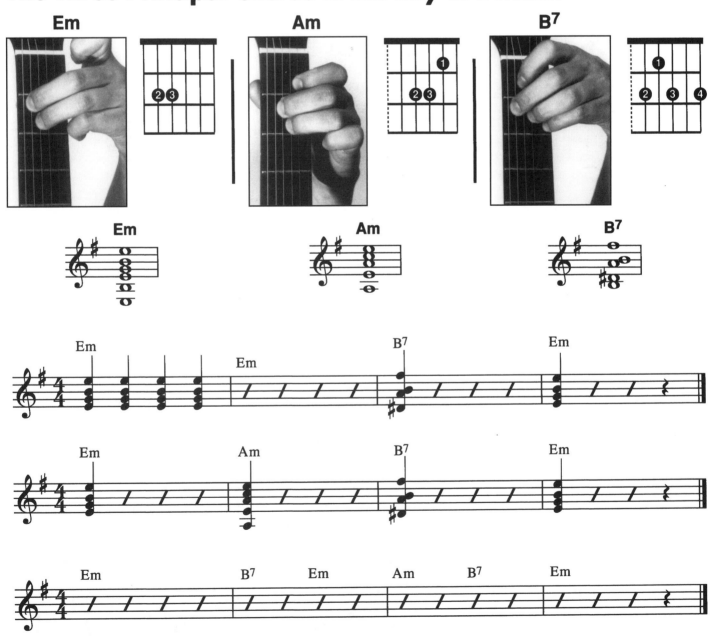

Etude in E Minor

COUNT: 1 & 2 & 3 & 4 &

Learn the melody and chords.

Joshua Fit the Battle

Gospel Tune

Moderately, with a beat

TEACHER: Em

Josh-ua fit the bat-tle of___ Jer-i-cho,___ Jer-i-cho,___

Jer-i-cho;___ Josh-ua fit the bat-tle of___ Jer-i cho___ and the

walls came tum-blin' down. (That morn-in')___ down.

You may talk a-bout your King of Gid-e-on, You may

talk a-bout your man of Saul, But there's none like good old

Josh-u-a___ at the bat-tle of Jer-i-cho.

*Remember to play from the beginning. Skip the 1st ending and end with the 2nd ending.

Alternating Bass Notes in the Key of F

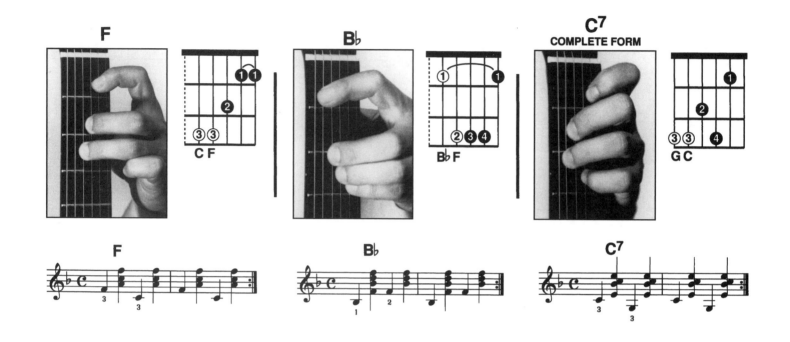

Accompaniment in F Major

Oh, My Darling Clementine
(Duet)

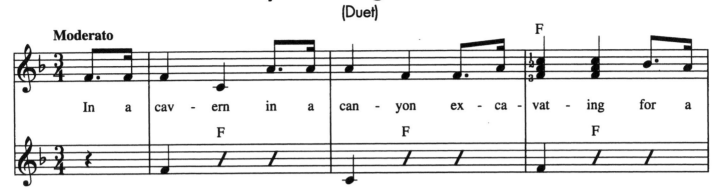

In a cav - ern in a can - yon ex - ca - vat - ing for a

mine, Dwelt a min - er for - ty - nin - er and his daugh - ter Clem - en -

tine. Oh my dar - ling, oh my dar - ling, oh my dar - ling Clem - en -

tine; You are lost and gone for - ev - er, dread - ful sor - ry, Clem - en - tine.

Shave and a Haircut

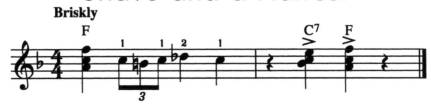

Before attempting this famous march by John Philip Sousa, you may want to review the discussion of 6/8 time on **page 95.**

The Liberty Bell
(Duet)

John Philip Sousa

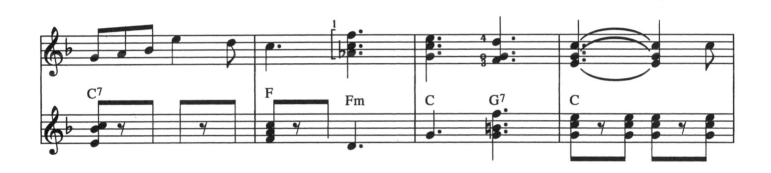

*The marcato accent (∧ or ∨) is a stressed accent.

Alexander's Ragtime Band

Solo or Duet

Irving Berlin

With a beat

VERSE: KEY OF C MAJOR

NOTE CHANGE OF KEY

CHORUS IN F MAJOR

Sixteenth Notes

Sixteenth notes are black notes with two flags added to the stems  or

Generally when two or more sixteenth notes are played, they are joined with two beams:

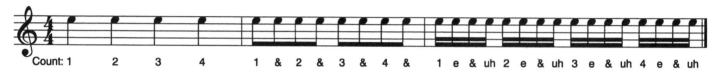

Sixteenth notes are played four to a beat, twice as fast as eighth notes and four times as fast as quarter notes. Use alternate picking when playing sixteenth notes.

4 quarter notes = 8 eighth notes = 16 sixteenth notes

In 2/4 time

In 3/4 time

Mixin' It Up

The pattern of an eighth note followed by two sixteenth notes is very common. The following song illustrates it. Watch the picking carefully.

The Happy Sailor

The rhythm of two sixteenth notes followed by an eighth note is also fairly common. Again, watch your picking carefully.

Variations on a Square Dance Tune

Dwight Yoakum is one of the few country artists to successfully cross over to rock. Starting in the 1980s, Yoakum acquired a devout following loyal to his brand of rootsy, blues-influenced music.

Photo: © Ken Settle

Introducing Arpeggios

When the notes of a chord are played in succession it is an ARPEGGIO.

East Side, West Side

The Man on the Flying Trapeze

Optional 2nd part
for duet:

Scarborough Fair

(Duet)

This beautiful English folk song was a big hit for Simon and Garfunkel in the '60s. It is arranged here as a duet, and the student should learn both parts. Keep the arpeggios flowing smoothly in the second part with fingers held down as long as possible.

The Doo-Wop Ballad

In the 1950s a style of rock and roll ballad called "doo-wop" became very popular. This type of song featured many long held notes sung over an accompaniment of triplets, played either as chords or arpeggios. Here are a few samples of each.

Key of C (Chords)

The same chords played as arpeggios:

Important: Hold fingers down for the above arpeggios as long as possible

Key of G (Chords)

Arpeggios:

Key of C Chords, with bass notes

Key of C, with variations

Key of G Chords, with bass notes

Key of G, with variations

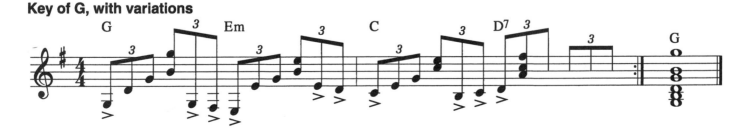

Here is a song written in '50s "doo-wop" style. Learn the melody and arpeggio-style accompaniment.

My Angel Baby

The Key of A Major

The key signature of three sharps indicates the key of A major. All F's are played as F♯, all C's are played as C♯, and all G's are played as G♯ unless otherwise indicated by a natural sign.

When learning the two-octave A major scale below, follow the fingering carefully. Like all scales, this one should be practiced daily.

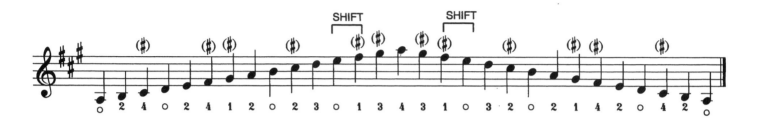

The Three Principal Chords in A with Bass Notes

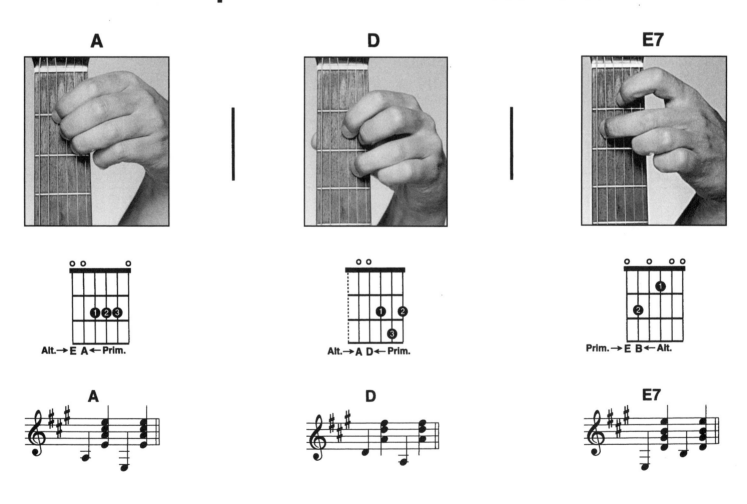

Accompaniments in A Major

Arpeggio Style

*Often referred to as "the guitar player's guitar player," **Joe Satriani** has been a mentor to the likes of Steve Vai and Metallica's Kirk Hammett. He is quietly one of the most respected guitarists of the 1980s and 1990s.*

Scale Etude in A Major

Arpeggio Etude

HOLD FINGERS IN PLACE AS LONG AS POSSIBLE

Hard, Ain't It Hard

Traditional

It's hard, and it's hard, ain't it hard to
love one that nev-er did love you. And it's
hard, ain't it hard, yes, it's hard, dear Lord, to
love one who nev-er could be true.

Hail, Hail, The Gang's All Here

Words: Anon.

Music: Sir Arthur Sullivan

Hail, hail,_____ the gang's all here;
What the heck do we care? What the heck do we care?
Hail, hail,_____ the gang's all here;
What the heck do we care now?

Sixteenth Note Studies in A Major

*Since the late 1970s, **Tom Petty** has been one of contemporary music's most enduring singer-songwriters. Petty, along with his group the Heartbreakers, has produced some of the most recognizable songs since the late 1970s, always managing to remain both current and classic.*

Chord Review

Before continuing further, make sure you know the following chords, their primary bass notes (roots) and alternate bass notes. You should also be able to recognize the chords when they are written out in notes.

Major Chords

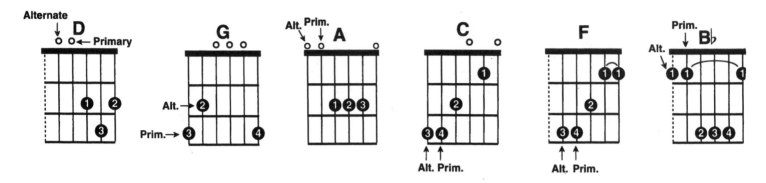

Minor Chords

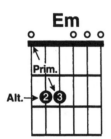
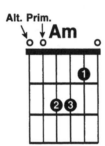
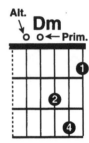

Seventh Chords

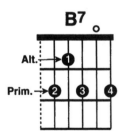
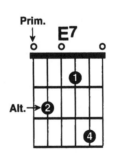
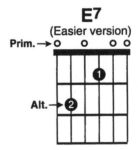
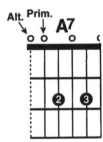

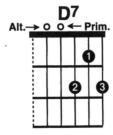
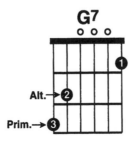
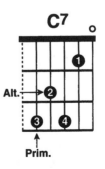

Chord Exercises

Make sure you can play the following chord exercises without missing a beat:

Key of C Major

Key of A Minor

Key of F Major

Key of E Minor

Key of G Major

Key of D Major

Key of C Major

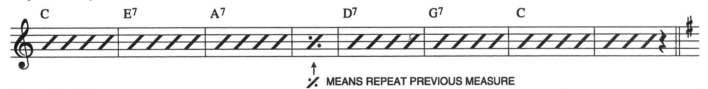

⤴ ⁒ MEANS REPEAT PREVIOUS MEASURE

Key of G Major

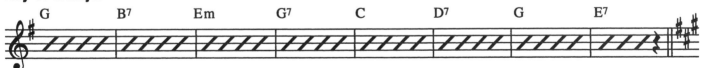

The above exercises can be played either:

1. Strumming once for each **/** (slash)

2. Substituting a primary bass note for the 1st beat of each measure

3. Substituting a primary bass note for the 1st beat of each measure and an alternate bass note for the 3rd beat of each measure.

Hammer-ons

The hammer-on effect is very common in today's music, especially in rock, heavy metal, country, blues and jazz. Every guitarist should be able to play this exciting technique. Hammer-on means playing a note by bringing a left-hand finger down hard enough to sound the note.

A hammer-on to a *fingered* string is done like this:

1. Start with the fingered note, the E on the 4th string, 2nd fret.

2. Strike the string with the pick while keeping the 1st finger firmly in place.

3. Then hammer the 2nd finger down hard and fast. The F will sound.

In musical notation, this is written:

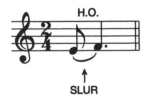

The curved line between the E and the F is called a slur and means that the F is not picked. The initials "H.O." above the staff stand for hammer-on. (Not all publications use this abbreviation.)

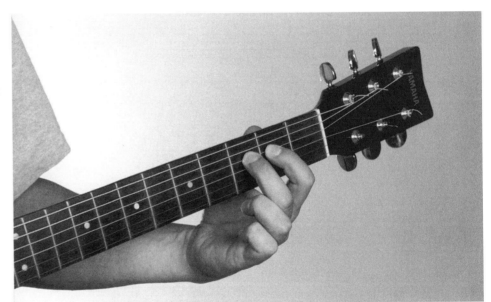

A hammer-on to an *open* string is done like this:

1. Strike the open A string with the pick.

2. Bring the 2nd finger down on the A string, 2nd fret, with a fast, hard, hammering motion and keep it there.

3. The note B will sound without picking the string a second time.

Here it is in music notation:

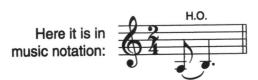

"John Hardy" and "Old Blue" are written in cut time (also called *alla breve*). The symbol for this is ₵, which means that the music is counted two beats to a measure. Every note value is cut by half: whole notes get two beats, half notes one beat, quarter notes a half beat each and so on.

John Hardy

Calypso

Calypso is Caribbean music of West African derivation. It was originally a means of social commentary sung over a rhythmic background and is a direct ancestor of today's rap music. A more Americanized type of calypso became popular in the '50s through the recordings of Harry Belafonte and others. These records featured the guitar in a prominent rhythmic role, but not usually as a solo instrument. Since most calypso songs use only a few chords, students can learn to play calypso music by mastering the rhythm pattern, called a strum.

To start, play the following strum:
(follow the picking carefully)

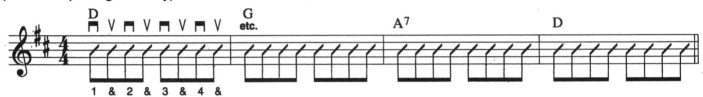

Now omit the beat played at 3

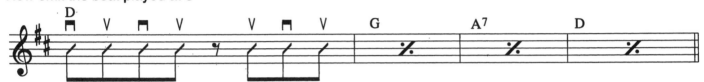

As you can see, the tricky part is leaving out the 3rd beat and playing the two up-picks in a row.

Here are some typical calypso chord progressions. Practice them until you can play them without missing a beat. Then try the song on the next page.

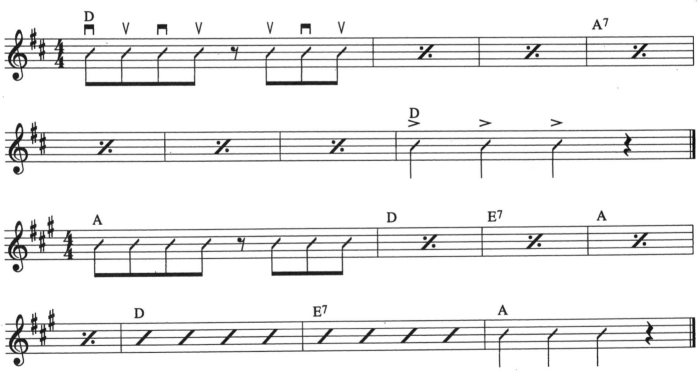

Occasionally the chord must be changed in the middle of a measure. When this happens, change on the "and" of 2, as in the example below:

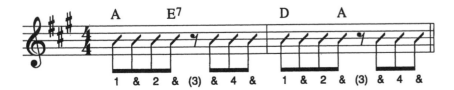

Hey Lolly Lolly

(Student to learn both the strum and solo parts)

Traditional calypso song

Hey lol - ly, lol - ly lol - ly, hey lol - ly, lol - ly lo,—

Hey lol - ly, lol - ly lol - ly, hey lol - ly, lol - ly lo.—

Fine

First you sing— a sim - ple line,— hey lol - ly, lol - ly lo,—

Then you try— and make it rhyme,— hey lol - ly, lol - ly lo.—

D.C. al Fine

The Sloop "John B."

Traditional calypso song

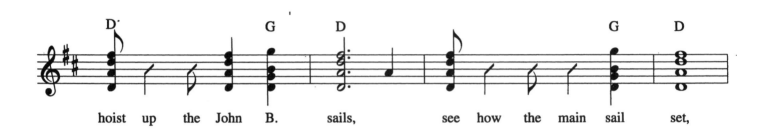

hoist up the John B. sails, see how the main sail set,

send for the cap-tain a - shore let— me go home.— Oh, let— me go

home,_____ please let— me go home,

feel so break— up, I wan-na go home.

The Key of D Minor

As you have already learned, the key signature of one flat signifies the key of F major. It can also indicate the key of D minor which is called the relative minor key of F major. The one flat in the key signature means that all B's are played as B♭ unless preceded by a natural sign.

Here are three different D minor scales. Follow the fingering carefully and add them to your daily practice routine.

The D Natural Minor Scale

The D Harmonic Minor Scale

The D Melodic Minor Scale

(Notice that when this scale descends the 6th and 7th notes of the scale are lowered a half step.)

The Three Principal Chords in D Minor with Bass Notes

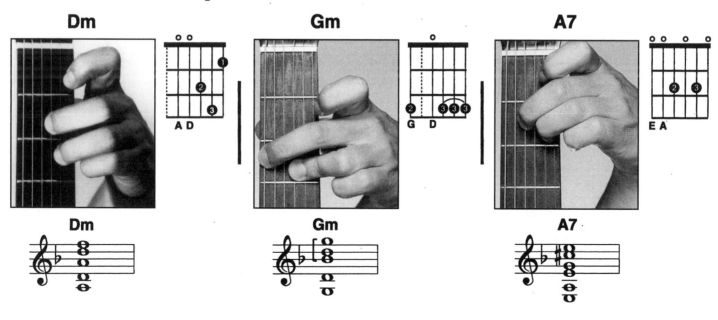

140

Sicilian Tarantella

A tarantella is a fast dance of Italian origin that supposedly mimics the movements of someone who has been bitten by a tarantula. This tarantella is very popular and is often performed at Italian weddings. The arrangement uses both the D minor and the F major scales. Remember that all Bs are flat. Then create an accompaniment using the indicated chords.

*Starting in the late 1980s and continuing into the 2000s, Green Day, with charismatic frontman **Billie Joe Armstrong**, aims to revive the raw energy of the original 1970s punk bands. The band is still making a mark and carving out its own niche in rock music.*

The House of the Rising Sun

(Duet in E Minor—student to learn both parts)

Traditional

Slow and bluesy

HOLD CHORDS WHEREVER POSSIBLE

Sixteenth Notes and 6/8 Time

As in 2/4, 3/4 and 4/4 time, in 6/8 time sixteenth notes are played twice as fast as eighth notes. Compare the following:

The old folk song "House of the Rising Sun" became a big hit in the 1960s using this accompaniment in 6/8 time. This accompaniment may be used with the arrangement of "House of the Rising Sun" on page 142. (Hold chords as much as possible.)

The Key of E Major

The key signature of four sharps indicates the key of E major. Although at first the student may find the number of sharps confusing, it is well worth the effort to master this key, because it is the key in which the guitar sounds best. Many of the best-known blues, country, folk and rock songs are in the key of E for this reason.

The key signature of four sharps means that all F's are played as F♯, all C's are played as C♯, all G's are played as G♯ and all D's are played as D♯. That is, all the sharps in the key of A plus D♯.

When learning the two-octave E major scale below, follow the fingering carefully. Like all scales this one should be practiced daily.

The Three Principal Chords in E with Bass Notes

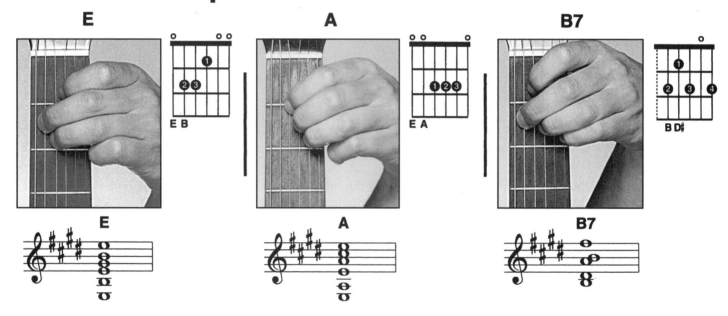

Accompaniments in E Major

Finger Exercise in E

A valuable exercise for the 2nd and 4th fingers. Remember that F, C, G and D are sharp.

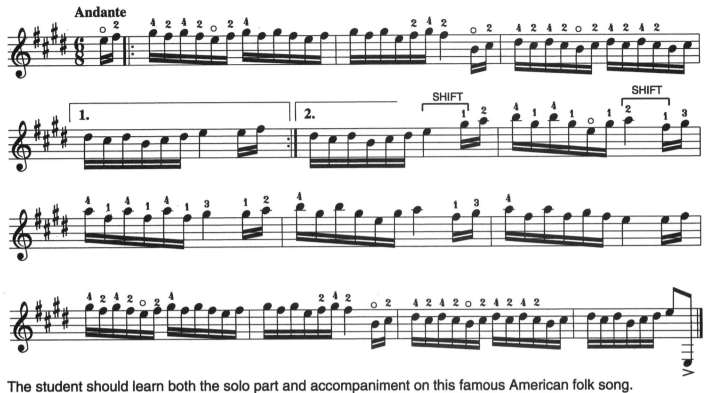

The student should learn both the solo part and accompaniment on this famous American folk song.

The Blue Tail Fly

In part 1, called the verse, each chord should be strummed once where it appears. Tempo is free in this part.

In part 2, called the chorus or refrain, play a perky bass/chord accompaniment similar to the one in 2/4 time on the preceding page.

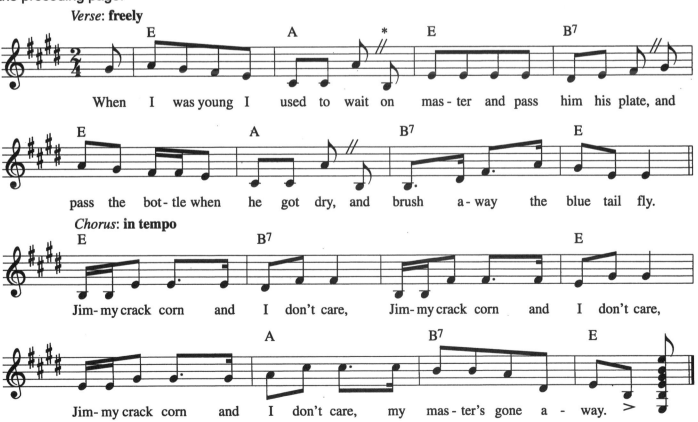

* This mark (//) is called a caesura in classical music. Pop musicians call them railroad tracks. They mean to leave an extra pause between the two notes.

Using Passing Notes in the Bass

As you have learned on previous pages, the bass/chord style of accompaniment is generally more effective than just strumming a chord on each beat. The bass notes used are the root (or name of the chord), the 5th and sometimes the 3rd of the chord. The chart below shows the various choices of bass note for every chord that you've learned.

Name of Chord	Root	5th	3rd
C	C	G	E
C7	C	G	E
F	F	C	A
G	G	D	B
G7	G	D	B
G minor	G	D	B♭
D	D	A	F♯
D7	D	A	F♯
D minor	D	A	F
A	A	E	C♯
A7	A	E	C♯
A minor	A	E	C
E	E	B	G♯
E7	E	B	G♯
E minor	E	B	G
B7	B	F♯	D♯

Generally the root should be your first choice, although when playing 7th chords it is often more effective to use an alternate note first. Your second choice can be dictated by how easy it is to get to it. For example, the note E in a C chord is the 3rd of that chord; it is easier to get to than the 5th (the note G).

Using Passing Notes in the Bass (cont'd.)

It is sometimes effective to use passing notes to connect the ordinary bass notes of a chord. Passing notes are notes that do not belong to the chord, but connect the notes that do belong to it (the root, 5th or 3rd) usually by step. Here are some examples of various styles.

Diminished Chords

So far all the chords you have learned belong to three different families: major, minor and seventh. Another type of chord common in jazz, classical and pop music is the diminished chord. Diminished chords can be derived from ordinary 7th chords **by flatting every note in the 7th chord except the root.**

D7

For example, starting with D7, we have the notes D (root), F♯ (3rd), A (5th) and C (7th).

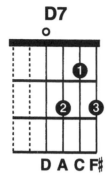

D A C F♯

D dim.

To make a D7 into a D diminished chord, flat the 3rd, 5th, and 7th a half step or one fret. This gives us the notes D, F A♭, and C♭ (or B).

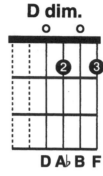

D A♭ B F

A7

Starting with A7, we have A (root), C♯ (3rd), E (5th) and G (7th).

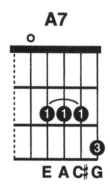

E A C♯ G

A dim.

To make an A7 into an A diminished chord, flat the 3rd, 5th, and 7th a half step. This gives us the notes A, C, E♭, and G♭ (or F♯).

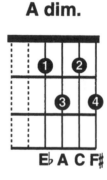

E♭ A C F♯

E7

Starting with E7, we have E (root), G♯ (3rd), B (5th) and D (7th).

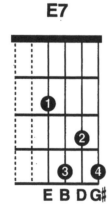

E B D G♯

E dim.

To make an E7 into an E diminished chord, flat the 3rd, 5th, and 7th a half step. This gives us the notes E, G, B♭, and D♭ (or C♯).

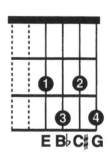

E B♭ C♯ G

The good news is that these three diminished chords can be used for every diminished chord in music:

D dim.	=	F dim.	=	A♭ or G♯ dim.	=	B dim.	
A dim.	=	C dim.	=	E♭ or D♯ dim.	=	G♭ or F♯ dim.	
E dim.	=	G dim.	=	B♭ dim.			=	D♭ or C♯ dim.

For a bass note, pick any low note in the diminished chord that moves smoothly to your next bass note.

You Tell Me Your Dream

(Solo with Diminished Chords)

Moderate Dixieland jazz tempo

You had a dream, well,

I had one, too.

I know mine's best 'cause it

was of you.

Come, sweet - heart, tell me,

now is the time:

You tell me your dream,

I'll tell you mine.

Pull-offs

The pull-off effect is very common in all types of music, but especially in rock, heavy metal, country, blues and jazz. Like the hammer-on (see page 134), the pull-off allows you to play a note without using the right hand.

A pull-off to a *fingered* string is done like this:

1. Start with a fingered note, the G on the 1st string, 3rd fret.

2. Pick the 1st string with the 1st and 3rd fingers on F and G.

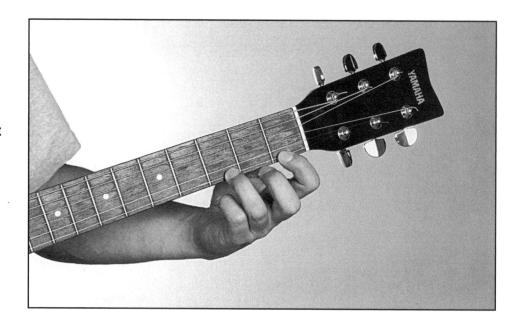

3. Pull the 3rd finger off the string with a lateral motion so that the F sounds clearly.

In musical notation, this is written:

The curved line between the G and the F is a slur which means that the F is not picked. The initials P.O. stand for pull-off, but not all publications use this notation.

A pull-off to an *open* string is done like this:

1. Start with a fingered note, as an example, the G on the 1st string, 3rd fret.

2. Pick the 1st string with the 3rd finger on G.

3. Pull the 3rd finger off the string using a lateral motion so that the open E sounds clearly.

Here it is in music notation:

Country Dance
(Study with Pull-offs)

Blues in A
(Study with Pull-offs and Hammer-ons)

The Polka
(Duet)

As its name implies, the polka was originally a Polish dance. It was brought to the United States in the 19th century and still enjoys great popularity. Polka albums are always among the top sellers regardless of other trends that may be popular. This polka is based on the folk song "Little Brown Jug."

Waylon Jennings (right) and **Willie Nelson's** (left) names are synonymous with traditional country music; but the two are also considered founders of the more contemporary, blues- and rock-influenced "Outlaw Sound." They remain two of the most dynamic, listened-to performers in the world.

Grace Notes

A grace note is a small note (usually an 8th note) with a slash mark through the flag placed before a normal-sized note, like this:

The grace note is played very light and fast (not accented) just before the regular note.

On the guitar, grace notes are played three different ways:

1. From below, as a quick hammer-on using two fingers

2. From above, as a quick pull-off using two fingers

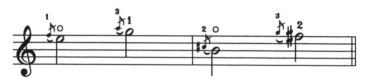

3. From either below or above, as a quick slide (see page 158) from a grace note to the regular note using one finger.

Grace notes can be very effective in adding sparkle to a melody, and guitarists like them because they sound good and are easy to play. Although it would be possible to play grace notes before every note in a melody, this would soon become an irritating mannerism, and the tasteful player will limit the use of grace notes to a few effective places.

Amazing Grace Notes

In the following study play the grace notes whichever way is most comfortable and the way they sound best to you.

Colonel Bogey

This great march became popular after its use in the movie classic "The Bridge on the River Kwai." Follow the fingering carefully on the grace notes.

Kenneth J. Alford

NOTE: E♯ IS THE SAME AS F♮, 1st STRING, 1st FRET

Augmented Chords

To augment something means to make it larger. In music, an augmented chord is one in which the interval from the root to the 5th has been made larger by a half step.

C Major

For example, starting with the C major chord, we have the notes C (root), E (3rd) and G (5th).

C E G C E

C Aug

To make a C major chord into a C augmented chord, raise the 5th a half step, to G♯.

C E G♯ C E

G Major

Starting with a G major chord, we have G (root), B (3rd) and D (5th).

G B D G B G

G Aug

To make a G major chord into a G augmented chord, raise the 5th a half step, to D♯.

G B D♯ G B G

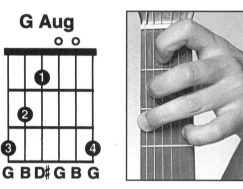

F Major

Starting with an F major chord, we have F (root), A (3rd) and C (5th).

F A C F

F Aug

To make an F major chord into an F augmented chord, raise the 5th a half step, to C♯.

F A C♯ F

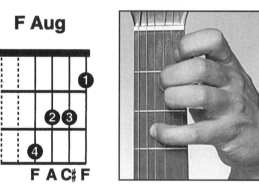

D Major

Starting with a D major chord, we have D (root), F♯ (3rd) and A (5th).

D A D F♯

D Aug

To make a D major chord into a D augmented chord, raise the 5th a half step, to A♯.

D A♯ D F♯

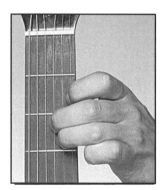

The good news is that these four chords can be used for every augmented chord in music:

C augmented	=	E augmented	=	G♯ or A♭ augmented
G augmented	=	B augmented	=	D♯ or E♭ augmented
F augmented	=	A augmented	=	C♯ or D♭ augmented
D augmented	=	F♯ augmented	=	A♯ or B♭ augmented

Augmented Chords (cont'd.)

Augmented chords are almost unknown in rock, blues and folk music, but are greatly used in jazz and pop songs prior to the rock era. The following chord progressions are typical of the way augmented chords are used.

IMPORTANT: In modern sheet music, augmented chords are usually indicated by a plus sign (for example C+, G+ and so on).

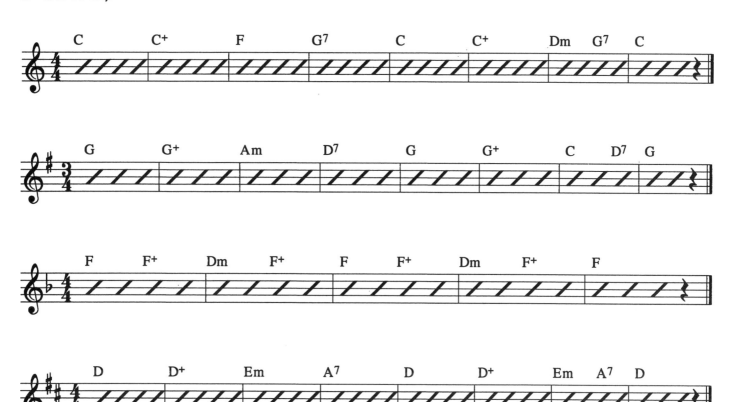

The following chord progression fits the melody of the great Duke Ellington standard *Take the A Train*. Note the extensive use of augmented chords.

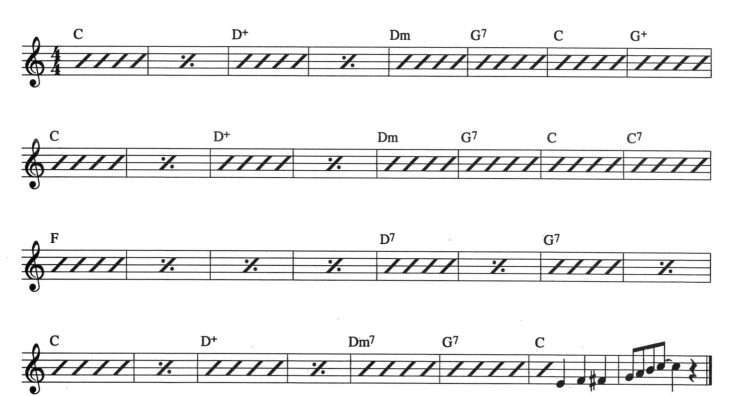

Slides and How To Play Them

Sliding up to or away from a note is an effective device that is much used by today's guitar players.

1. Sliding from one note to another. This must always be done on one string, either up or down. Finger the first note and pick the string. Then, without releasing the pressure on the string, slide to the next note.

In musical notation:

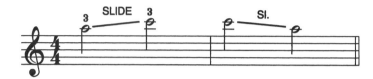

2. Often the slide begins on an indefinite note a few frets above or below the final note. Start with a little pressure on the string, but not enough to press it down to the fret. Then, as you slide toward the final note, gradually increase the pressure so that when you reach the final note it sounds clear.

3. Sliding away from a definite note to an indefinite note is more or less the reverse of #2 above. Start with any note that is at least five frets up the fingerboard. Pick the string, and as you slide down and away from the note, gradually release the pressure on the string so that your finger stops its vibration.

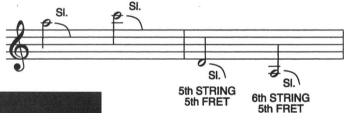

5th STRING
5th FRET

6th STRING
5th FRET

Photo: © Ken Settle

Bonnie Raitt *writes and performs music deeply rooted in the American classics: country, blues and rock. Her sound features an earthy vocal style and superb slide-guitar playing. She has amassed a loyal following throughout the 1980s and 1990s.*

Slidin' Around
(Duet)

This duet demonstrates the use of slides in blues playing. For best results, the student should learn both parts. If playing alone, play the 2nd part first, then the 1st part, then the 2nd part again to finish up. If playing as a duet, have the 2nd player play the arrangement through once, then add the top part. More advanced players will want to improvise some blues against the funky bass line.

Devil's Dream Hornpipe

Our Katie

(Oberek)*

*An oberek (o-BED-ek) is a lively Polish dance.

Abide with Me
(Duet)

This arrangement of the lovely old hymn combines a chord/melody solo in the 1st part with an arpeggio-style accompaniment in the 2nd part. The student should learn both parts. Also note that the accompaniment is always played at a dynamic one level lower than the melody part.

Words by Henry Francis Lyte

Music by William H. Monk

HOLD FINGERS DOWN AS LONG AS POSSIBLE

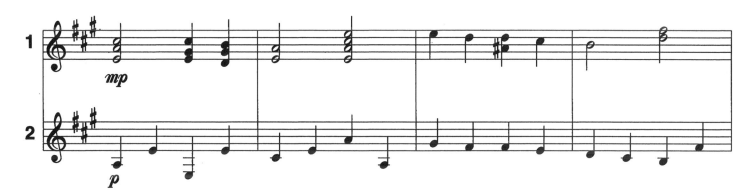

Lento means to play slowly.

Bends or Chokes

The laws of acoustics state that when the tension of a string is increased, its pitch rises. Blues players discovered this at least a hundred years ago, and the technic now called "bending" or "choking" a string has become a standard part of the modern guitarist's bag of tricks. Here's how to do it:

1. Finger any note on any of the first five strings and pick the string. Take, for example, the note E on the 2nd string, 5th fret.

2. Keeping the pressure on the string, push it across the fingerboard till you hear the pitch rise a half step, from E to F

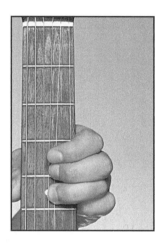

Bends do not work too well on the lower frets, so make sure the note you're bending is at least on the 3rd fret or higher. Also make sure you're using a light-gauge string. It's difficult to do this effect if the string is too stiff.

Modern heavy metal players often bend notes a whole step, 1-1/2 steps and even 2 steps higher. This can be accomplished by using an extremely light gauge string—.008s—and playing up around the 12th fret.

When bending notes on the low E, the string must be *pulled* to avoid pushing it off the fingerboard.

Playing A on the 6th string, 5th fret.

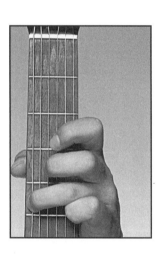

Bending A to an A♯

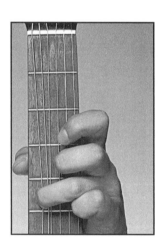

Unfortunately for the student, the notation of this effect is still in contention. Some arrangers write the *fingered* note and indicate by using an arrow that it should be bent up a 1/2 step or more. Others prefer to write the *final* pitch with a notation to bend it up from a lower note. In this book we use the former notation.

Bending the Blues

Pistol Pete

* The arrow with 1/4 above it is often used to mean: Pull the note up a quarter of a step, that is, not quite up to the next note. One advantage that guitar players have over piano players is that they can play these sounds that do not exist on a piano.

Counterpoint

The word "counterpoint" means playing two or more melodies at the same time. Of course, the idea is that they sound good together. In classical music the unquestioned master of counterpoint was the great J.S. Bach (1685–1750) who thought nothing of *improvising* four- and five-part fugues. Counterpoint hasn't been used much in popular music, but occasionally a little gem turns up, like *Simple Melody* by Irving Berlin.

In this one, he manages to write two different melodies that sound good individually or when played simultaneously. The following arrangement can be played in several ways. Either of the parts marked 1 and 2 can be played as a solo or as a solo accompanied by part 3. Or, all three parts can be played simultaneously.

Simple Melody

Words and Music by Irving Berlin

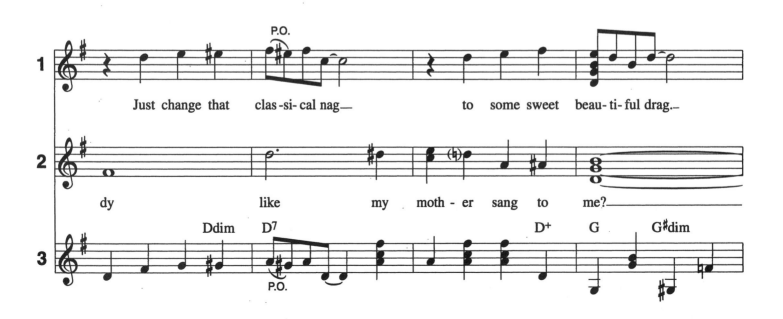

If you will play from a cop - y of a tune that is chop - py you'll get

One with good old fash - ioned

D⁷   G   D⁷   G

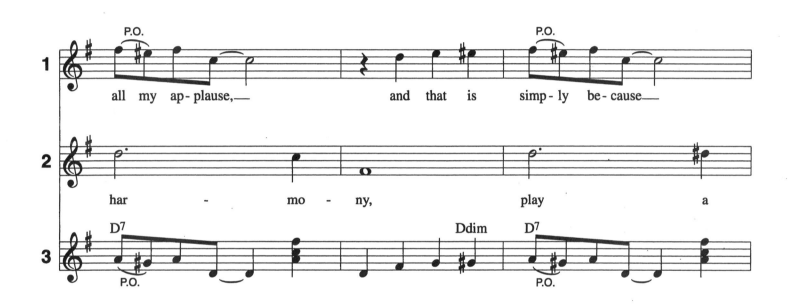

all my ap - plause,___ and that is simp - ly be - cause___

har - mo - ny, play a

D⁷   Ddim   D⁷

I want to lis - ten to rag.___

sim - ple mel - o - dy.

No chords   G

The last technique described in this book combines pull offs and hammer ons in ways that are used by today's hottest rock, blues and jazz guitarists. Concentrate on articulating clearly. That is, make sure each note sounds clear regardless of whether or not it is picked.

Chord Accompaniment Guide

Key	The Three Principal Chords			The Relative Minor Chords			Alternate Chords					
	I	IV	V7	i	iv	V7						
A♭	A♭	D♭	E♭7	Fm	B♭m	C7	A♭6	A♭dim.	A♭aug.	D♭6	Fm6	B♭m6
A	A	D	E7	F#m	Bm	C#7	A6	Adim.	Aaug.	D6	F#m6	Bm6
B♭	B♭	E♭	F7	Gm	Cm	D7	B♭6	B♭dim.	B♭aug.	E♭6	Gm6	Cm6
B	B	E	F#7	A♭m	D♭m	E♭7	B6	Bdim.	Baug.	E6	G#m6	C#m6
C	C	F	G7	Am	Dm	E7	C6	Cdim.	Caug.	F6	Am6	Dm6
D♭	D♭	G♭	A♭7	B♭m	E♭m	F7	D♭6	D♭dim.	D♭aug.	G♭6	B♭m6	E♭m6
D	D	G	A7	Bm	Em	F#7	D6	Ddim.	Daug.	G6	Bm6	Em6
E♭	E♭	A♭	B♭7	Cm	Fm	G7	E♭6	E♭dim.	E♭aug.	A♭6	Cm6	Fm6
E	E	A	B7	C#m	F#m	G#7	E6	Edim.	Eaug.	A6	C#m6	F#m6
F	F	B♭	C7	Dm	Gm	A7	F6	Fdim.	Faug.	B♭6	Dm6	Gm6
F#	F#	B	C#7	E♭m	A♭m	B♭7	F#6	F#dim.	F#aug.	B6	D#m6	G#m6
G	G	C	D7	Em	Am	B7	G6	Gdim.	Gaug.	C6	Em6	Am6

Guitar Fingerboard Chart
Frets 1–12

STRINGS

6th	5th	4th	3rd	2nd	1st
E	A	D	G	B	E

Fretboard note names (strings 6th–1st):

FRETS	6th	5th	4th	3rd	2nd	1st
Open	E	A	D	G	B	E
1st Fret	F	A#/B♭	D#/E♭	G#/A♭	C	F
2nd Fret	F#/G♭	B	E	A	C#/D♭	F#/G♭
3rd Fret	G	C	F	A#/B♭	D	G
4th Fret	G#/A♭	C#/D♭	F#/G♭	B	D#/E♭	G#/A♭
5th Fret	A	D	G	C	E	A
6th Fret	A#/B♭	D#/E♭	G#/A♭	C#/D♭	F	A#/B♭
7th Fret	B	E	A	D	F#/G♭	B
8th Fret	C	F	A#/B♭	D#/E♭	G	C
9th Fret	C#/D♭	F#/G♭	B	E	G#/A♭	C#/D♭
10th Fret	D	G	C	F	A	D
11th Fret	D#/E♭	G#/A♭	C#/D♭	F#/G♭	A#/B♭	D#/E♭
12th Fret	E	A	D	G	B	E